AFTER-DEATH
COMMUNICATION

EMMA HEATHCOTE-JAMES

AFTER-DEATH COMMUNICATION

Hundreds of true stories from the UK of people
who have communicated with their loved ones

metro

Published by Metro Publishing Ltd,
3, Bramber Court, 2 Bramber Road,
London W14 9PB, England

www.blake.co.uk

First published in paperback in 2004

ISBN 1 84358 122 1

British Library Cataloguing-in-Publication Data:

A catalogue record for this book is available from the British Library.

Design by www.envydesign.co.uk

Printed in Great Britain by Bookmarque Ltd, Croydon, Surrey

1 3 5 7 9 10 8 6 4 2

Papers used by Metro Publishing are natural, recyclable products made from
wood grown in sustainable forests. The manufacturing processes conform to the
environmental regulations of the country of origin.

*Dedicated with love to Mum and Dad
and with fond memories and appreciation
to Gran and Gramps Giles*

'ONE OF THE GREATEST PAINS TO HUMAN
NATURE IS THE PAIN OF A NEW IDEA'

WALTER BAGEHOT

CONTENTS

ACKNOWLEDGEMENTS *xi*

PREFACE *1*

FOREWORD *7*
by Judy Guggenheim

INTRODUCTION 13

Grief and ADCs 16
ADCs and the Guggenheims 18
What is an ADC? 19
Other Research 22
Increasing Belief in the Afterlife 25
Questions 26
Truth v Reality 29

1. THE POINT OF DEATH 31

Death-bed Visions 31
Unprompted Appearances
of the Deceased 38
Remote ADCs 42
Wind 45
Light 50
Strange Feelings 52
Injury Dreams 53

2. TWILIGHT AND SLEEP-STATE ADCS 55

Insight 56
Dreams of Comfort 61
A Final Goodbye 67

3. MESSAGES FROM THE OTHER SIDE 73

Lost ... and Found 74
Reassurance over Current Events 77
Gloomy Predictions 79
General Messages 81
Sitting Tenants 83
'I'm OK' 85

4. SYMBOLISM AND SIGNS 89

General Signs 89
Butterflies 93

Wind or Forceful Energy 96
The Appearance of Objects 98
Clocks Stopping 102
Electricity and Lights 106

5. REUNIONS OUT OF THE BLUE 109

Bedtime Visions 109
Reunions around the House 113
Experiences away from
  the Home 116
Hugs 118
A Stroke or Touch 119

6. AUDITORY COMMUNICATIONS 123

7. SCENT FROM ABOVE 131

A Scented Passing 131
Scent ... to Inform of Death 133
Scent after Death 136

8. MESSAGES OF HOPE 141

Hospital Visitors 141
During Labour 144
Before an Operation 145
During Illness 148

9. GLIMPSING THE OTHER SIDE 151

Major Explanations of the
  Phenomena 153
Near-Death Experiences 154
Out-of-Body Experiences 157

10. PETS RETURN 167

Postscript 177
How Can the ADCs Be Utilised? 178
Final Thoughts 179
The Guggenheims' ADC Project 181
The ADC Research Federation 182

Bereavement Groups
  and Organisations 183
Pet Charities and Support
  Groups 200
Recommended ADC-related
  websites 201
Fictional ADCs in Movies 203
Fictional ADCs in Novels
  and Plays 209
Endnotes 219
Bibliography and Suggested
  Further Reading 223

PRAISE FOR AFTER-DEATH COMMUNICATION

'No doubt Emma's book will inspire many people, primarily because of its simplicity. It speaks directly to one's heart and reminds each person of what is important.'

BILL AND JUDY GUGGENHEIM OF THE ADC PROJECT

'Emma Heathcote-James has produced a superb and easy-to-read book. This book, a true gem in After-Death Communication research, is full of compelling evidence with a powerful message of hope: that our consciousness survives bodily death. This book may change how you think about After-Death Communication — but even more importantly, it may change how you live your life.'

DR. JEFFREY LONG, M.D.
AFTER DEATH COMMUNICATION RESEARCH FOUNDATION,
TAHOMA, WASHINGTON, U.S.A.

'I welcome this book as a thoughtful and intelligent contribution to the body of worthwhile literature on a very important subject. It cannot fail to stimulate enquiring minds everywhere.'

JOHN SAMSON, BBC BROADCASTER AND MEMBER OF THE
SOCIETY FOR PSYCHICAL RESEARCH

'Since the days when man first inhabited this world, he has been preoccupied with the next. We long for confirmation that our loved ones have lived on and communicate that fact to us. Here is the definitive book about After-Death Communication. Warm, uplifting and reassuring, it provides the very evidence we need that our loved ones are ever near.'

GLENNYCE ECKERSLEY, AUTHOR OF OUT OF THE BLUE AND ANGEL
AT MY SHOULDER, AND OTHERS.

'After-Death Communication *is thoroughly researched and beautifully written with the scientific mind and lovingly spiritual heart of Emma Heathcote-James. It's a truly comforting book for those who've experienced an After-Death Communication, and for those who wonder about life after death.'*
DOREEN VIRTUE, PH.D., AUTHOR OF *MESSAGES FROM YOUR ANGELS*
BOOK AND ORACLE CARDS

*'This fascinating book couldn't come at a better time –
this information has to get out there.'*
JACKY NEWCOMB, COLUMNIST OF *CHAT IT'S FATE!* MAGAZINE

'It's time to bring spirits into the mainstream where they can transform our chaotic lives and world. Emma does this with warmth and clarity.'
JILL WELLINGTON, CO-AUTHOR OF *FIREWORKS*

'Please now do for the etheric what you've done for the angels!'
CONTRIBUTOR

'Working as a doctor and research fellow, with an interest in complementary medicine, I am very interested in the understanding of spiritual realities and higher worlds touched upon in your [last] book. I am convinced that only a clear understanding of these realities will bring about real progress in medicine, psychology, religion and virtually all fields of human activity. That is why I am delighted that researchers like yourself are taking the trouble to investigate these unknown areas of human existence and make their findings available to a wider audience.'
READER

'Thank you for having the courage to produce something which is normally confined within university walls.'
CONTRIBUTOR

'I am so glad something so real and apparent is at last being studied seriously.'
CONTRIBUTOR

ACKNOWLEDGEMENTS

THE GREATEST THANKS MUST go to Judy and Bill Guggenheim for their support and endorsement of this book, and to Judy especially for your friendship and holding my hand throughout! In turn, a huge big thank-you to all the people whose voices are heard within these pages – if it wasn't for your letters and support this book would never have been born. That thanks extends to everyone else who has written, not just to share accounts, but to send words of encouragement – I really do appreciate your letters and they seem to arrive when I need them most!

Despite things moving on, I still acknowledge had it have not been for the support and encouragement of one very special person this book would never have made it past the opening paragraph. Paul, thank you for coming into my life when I needed you most – and equally for leaving it when we both needed to move forward. I will never forget all the fun, laughter and adventures we shared and most importantly your love and unconditional friendship. Much of this was written whilst we were together in Germany, and this book will always be a tangible reminder of that special time.

To my family and friends, primarily to Hector and the new addition, Mutley, for curling up at my side as I write and dragging me through the fields each day – thank you for being the most wonderful, consistent and faithful chaps in my life and for your companionship and unconditional love. To my parents and Dix for your love, care, support and persistence in putting up with me and thank you Andy Weekes, the Middletons and the Baylisses for putting up with them and being such wonderful family extensions! To those closer to home, Rob and Helen Davies, the Applebys, Ratamir Magdenovic, Nigel Smith, John Bluck, Nigel Stubbings, Hazel and Rod Attwood and all those who congregated in The Fleece... Whether you knew it or not, you were all really good company when writer's block set in and lifted me from hermit mode when it didn't! To you all, thank you all for listening and caring enough to pull me out of my cave for much-needed coffees, dog-walks, glasses of wine, dinners and long evenings in front of the fire – you are all such incredibly special neighbours and I am so glad you're all a part of my life.

Also, to my closest friends and work colleagues who all stuck by as this book evolved, and amid the revision as it went to paperback, to Pete and Jack Devonald, Lavinia Seaton-Smith, J-F, Anne Leigh, Joanie Spiegel, Sir Tim Ackroyd, Nick Plowright, Rhodri Williams, Lucy Ladbrooke, Alix West, Kate Philpot and Tess Loftus. I thank each of you for your continued friendship, fun, laughter and understanding my mania throughout another book. Thank you for always being there when I needed you and equally so for keeping out of the way when I didn't! I adore you all. To those I worked alongside whilst writing the early manuscripts, to Howard Belgard and all at BBC Radio Hereford and Worcester, Will and all at Hanrahan Media and on Star Lives, Sarah Walker and the cast and crew of 420 Seconds of Love – producing that film involved some of the best months of my life and has culminated in something I am deeply proud to have been a part of – thank you!

And to Marc Ilyffe who was a special friend and one whom I was immensely proud of – it just fills me with such sorrow that I write your name in here with loving memory and not in the paragraph above as the good friend that you were to me. I shall miss and never forget you mate and do feel privileged to have known you. I just pray that out of the tragedy the special friendship that has developed with your Mum and family will always remain.

Special mention as well to some fellow authoresses – I so appreciate your empathy, humour and numerous phone calls – it's so good to be reminded we're all in the same boat and not totally alone! To my dear friend Glennyce Eckersley, thank you for helping me so very much with this and every venture and to Doreen Virtue, Kate Boydell and Teresa Moorey for being on the sidelines with words of reassurance and for your genuine understanding of the rollercoaster ride that producing a manuscript involves!

Thank you as well to Victoria Piechowiak for going through another script with me, to Marianne Rankin for the conversations, laughter and lunches, to John and Clare Samson for being such fantastic and supportive friends, to The Society for Psychical Research, The Churches' Fellowship for Psychical and Spiritual Studies and The Alistair Hardy Trust for all showing an interest in this research, to Dave Thompson for opening my mind to explore more deeply what was touched on in this book and became the sole topic of my next – and to Dr Martin Stringer and Dr Gordon Lynch in the Theology Department at the University of Birmingham for sticking by!

Finally, to Gay Pilgrim for simply being the beautiful person that you are, for your care and support and for wading through a few of the early draft manuscripts. And of course to John and Rosie, Adam, James, Michelle, Lucian and all at Metro Publishing – you know how much I appreciate your help and vision for turning yet more of my files of letters and reams of scrawled notes into the book you are now holding...

PREFACE

'Only three things are certain: death, taxes
and fear of both of them'

Woody Allen

T HE IDEA OF LIFE AFTER death – heaven, an afterlife,
spirits, ghosts and angels is not just problematical for science
but for the average human being as well. It is a topic guaranteed
to stir opinions, be they sceptical, blinkered, open-minded or
knowing. Like politics, religion should never be discussed
around the dinner table, but the thing with death – be you
religious or not, is that it affects every single one of us and, I am
sure, has been thought about at some point in each of our lives.
Nonetheless, the controversies have spiralled around for
hundreds, even thousands, of years and it doesn't seem as
though there is any real sign of things being resolved in the
immediate future. However, certain shifts have been and are
taking place. Slowly, as a race we are becoming more open-
minded and accepting. Today, in the twenty-first century, a shift
is taking place, one, I would argue, that is taking us away from
science being the be all and end all, and into a more spiritual
dimension. Anthropologically speaking, we have developed
through differing eras – one of magic, followed by religion and

then science – each one overlapping as the next is created. I would argue that here and now we are in the process of leaving the scientific era and heading towards a more spiritual outlook. Because of this, people are more willing to accept that some things do, indeed, defy logical answers and that science does not and cannot provide us, contemporaneously, with answers for everything.

It is worth noting that there has been a definite shift in the cultural climate engendering such experiences. Over the past two decades, there has been a growing 'New Age' movement that has redirected people's attentions towards spiritual matters. Many top paperback publishers increased their number of New Age-type books between the late Seventies and late Eighties – for some, Mind, Body and Spirit books have become their fastest-growing line of non-fiction books.' Walk into any book shop and you can see – topics that once were confined to being stuffed in a corner now have their own rapidly growing dedicated sections!

The whole area of religion in its varying forms – from origination to its future – has always fascinated me. Over the past ten years I have been fortunate enough to study both religious and numinous (spiritual) experiences involving angels, the Blessed Virgin Mary and Jesus, as well as looking into stigmata, cults, simulacra and, more recently, psychics and physical mediumship.

With regards to my own personal beliefs, I have not had any kind of first-hand experience myself, aside from a weeping icon in Egypt which isn't something I would necessarily term numinous. In no way am I evangelising about experiences, neither have I had a vision or voice telling me that this is my chosen path, although I do find it inexplicable that so many things have continued to come together leading me through a study of my own understanding through other people's spiritual experiences. Put simply, I am just creating a book by the people for the people. A book, I feel, needs to be published if only to make a point and show there is so much going on here which needs to be explored more fully. ADCs and religious experiences are not the type of thing which can be or indeed are discussed freely, even in today's environment – stigmas are still apparent and they in turn isolate people who have had such incredible experiences into believing they are on their own, and they most certainly are not.

Gathering evidence of loved ones surviving death via psychics and mediums has been a well-documented and argued debate for years and one which has interested me more and more over recent months. To get proof (with scientific back-up) of survival after death is something equally fascinating, and increasingly is becoming something I do believe is possible as the next research project I have planned will hopefully show. However, the material presented in this book is totally different and aside from all this. Accounts shared in here have nothing to do with psychics, clairvoyants or mediums, rather they are from ordinary people like you and me who have had some kind of spontaneous and non-induced experience of communication with the dead or, as coined by the Guggenheims, an After-Death Communication – an 'ADC'.

The Introduction offers a brief overview of what an ADC is, the work of the Guggenheims' ADC Project and other research which has been carried out into the phenomena, as well as belief traits in life after death. The subsequent chapters then deal with the actual accounts themselves, and various forms of witnessed and reported ADCs.

Unlike writing any other literary work, with this kind of book I think it is only fair, and perhaps a necessity, to lay out my views and stance on all of this from the outset – indeed, writing on such matters one is bound to have judgements, beliefs and bias which could interfere with the end result. I really hope mine have not.

My background is in the Anglo-Catholic tradition, from which I went on to spend six years studying theology and the sociology and anthropology of religion at university. I stress that I do not call myself religious in either the orthodox or practising

3

sense, though I do believe in something and acknowledge that I still have much to learn. I take a great deal from The Spiritual Laws and truths contained in Kahil Gibran's *The Prophet* and M Scott Peck's *The Road Less Travelled* and poetry such as Oriah Mountain Dreamer's *The Invitation* inspires me a great deal – I believe in a God, though for want of a better word, believe God is more of a Force. Indeed, I am continually fascinated by the fact that greater understanding of these diverse spiritual experiences and writings serves only to reinforce the underlying doctrine of most of the traditional world religions and the sad part of this for me is that the spirituality seems to have been lost and solely the dogma remains. Survival after death intrigues me and as I have delved more and more into the subject my beliefs are becoming more are more cemented in the fact I do not believe earthly bodily death is the end. And perhaps more reassuringly my fear of it has been increasingly lessened.

I am both aware and enraged how scientific and philosophical thought today seems to exalt the worldly and the material at the expense of the spiritual. Yes, there is a significant shift taking place, and people's eyes are slowly being opened, but such topics are still viewed by many with disrepute and as a result have annoyingly received scant attention and research. I believe there is a lot we do not know or understand and I am certainly not ashamed to admit that. I think it is important to keep an open mind, and one of the reasons why I have studied and written about this subject is to try and fill the gap. Few 'academics' like to put their names to the paranormal for fear of ridicule, and few academics write accessible books for the public. I do passionately feel it is important to broach these topics and write a layman's book. Indeed, academic books have their place, as do religious books, and this will, hopefully, start to fill the void in between. I write as if I were sitting on the fence and intend never to let my beliefs interfere with my work. My aim is to present you with the evidence and witness accounts I have had sent to me and let you, the reader, make up your own mind.

Now, the question with life after death and ADCs, as with any type of experience, is not whether or not the phenomenon can be proven or disproved. 'Elementary Dr Watson,' as Sir Arthur Conan Doyle's Sherlock Holmes character used to say. 'When you eliminate the impossible, whatever remains, no matter how improbable must be the truth.'

Only it is not quite as simple as it sounds. It is a known fact that it is an impossibility to replicate spontaneous phenomena in order to study it by way of scientific method. Sceptics may laugh – but a spontaneous, non-induced occurrence is just that ... spontaneous and non-induced. Instead, the issue is: what are we to do with the experiences?

We have two choices – either to dismiss them, close the book and say they are one-off, mind-projected hallucinations, a product of grief and wishful thinking; or we can share them, take from them and maintain an open mind. It is the latter I personally have chosen.

Some experiences are not grief-induced – some occur before the recipient even knows the person has died! I sincerely hope that this collection of experiences will help to break down some of the barriers and taboos which still surround death and grief and that the thoughts and sentiments in these pages will assist some with their loss.

Many who have written and, indeed, those of you reading who can identify with such accounts, may well be surprised at the similarities of yours with others. If nothing else, I hope this book communicates just how common these experiences are.

You are not alone.

And, no, as has been asked in countless letters, you most certainly are not going mad ...

FOREWORD

By Judy Guggenheim,
The ADC Project and co-author of
Hello from Heaven!

WHO WOULD HAVE THOUGHT in 1988, when Bill
Guggenheim and I began our original research, that direct
and spontaneous communications from our deceased loved ones
would finally have a name – After-Death Communications! These
sacred personal spiritual experiences have been with us since the
dawn of humankind, yet were often left in the shadows of
superstition and cultural lore for eons of time. But now, we can
speak freely with one another about ADCs, not having to fear
that our direct and personal contact from deceased loved ones
will be interpreted by others, including mental health
professionals, as bereavement fantasies, wishful thinking or,
worse, hallucinations. Emma Heathcote-James has led the way
for the people of the United Kingdom to further ADC research,
with compelling first-hand accounts from those eager to share
these wondrous experiences of contact *from* a deceased loved one.

You see, too many people have already acknowledged having
at least *one* ADC in their lifetime for us to any longer deny their
reality worldwide, regardless of their cultural, religious or non-

religious background. That's wonderful news. That means that ADCs are not only cross-cultural, but cross-dimensional too.

It is an honour for me to be co-founder and co-researcher of The ADC Project, thanks to the courage and determination of Bill Guggenheim, my former husband, who meticulously collected over 3,300 first-hand accounts in preparation for our breakthrough book, *Hello From Heaven!*. Dear Bill had always been an avid collector, and he found his life's calling in this very measured pursuit! Our North America collection has since grown to over 10,000 accounts from people *all* over the world, thanks to postal mail and Internet submissions. Soon, The ADC Project research will be at home at the University of Virginia, providing a world-wide database available to both experiencers as well as fellow researchers.

ADCs are often well-remembered from a childhood encounter that perhaps went unacknowledged, up to and including our own death-bed visions. In fact, it's conservatively estimated one-third of our world population has already experienced an after-death communication without the use of a psychic, medium, ritual or device, such as a séance or Ouiji board. Now, thats a lot of people from all corners and creases of this blue planet!

The ADC Project, for both Bill and myself, has never been about selling books, but about awakening souls, reminding us all where we came from and where we are going on this journey we call Life. It's all about remembering that we are all spiritual beings who are only temporarily on this planet to interact and to learn and teach our spiritual lessons. It's about re-awakening to *who* we truly are.

No doubt Emma's book will inspire many people, primarily because of its simplicity. It speaks directly to one's heart and reminds each person of what is important. It speaks loudly and clearly of love and the essential human qualities of compassion and forgiveness. *After-Death Communication*'s messages will bypass the selective rational mind and stir the memories within the soul. Those who read this book thoughtfully will be deeply moved by its simple truth.

After-Death Communication is about hope, not merely comfort for the bereaved. It provides a framework and an understanding of the vastness of the spiritual dimension, expanding our minds to see a larger wider reality, one that exists before birth and beyond physical death. Yet, you are also about to read a practical guide that can be interpreted on both simple and advanced levels of understanding, for it satisfies each reader where we are in our spiritual journey.

For some, it will be enough to know that we are still in contact with and connected to those we have loved and seemingly lost. For others, it will be a window through which we may glimpse a far vaster reality of not only life after physical death, but of a larger greater plan that is endless, eternal.

Many will doubt the reality of these ADC accounts, which is understandable within the context of not yet having one's own *direct* experience. But, no one else can offer the proof another requires. Only a *direct* experience, such as an ADC, NDE, OBE or angel encounter, can be someone's individualised and personal *proof*. Regrettably, the rest of us, including researchers, must declare these accounts as only *evidence* that consciousness survives physical death. We're all determining our own reality through direct experience, and *only* through direct experience, whether we're conscious of that process or not.

And if you've already recognised receiving an ADC encounter, then you no longer have to hope or wish for one. You already *know* in the belly of your being that you and all others survive their physical death. And you realise that there is no death, only the illusion of passing from one form into another form, moving to a familiar yet different vibration of energy and consciousness. A sense of 'going Home' for many, where you will be greeted to your time of passing by all those you have loved and lost to the illusion we call 'death'. Therefore, you need no longer doubt or question your perspective. You have already confirmed this through your own direct experience, an ADC. What a gift you have given yourself, freeing you to live your life more passionately, no longer fearing your own death! It's really that simple for each of us in determining our own reality.

Your life has more purpose and direction now, because you not only don't fear death, but you more fully embrace life. You find more meaningfulness in small moments, as you begin to awaken to your own personal truth and life path. The absence of the fear of death leaves a wondrous void in our psyche, one we can fill with more loving relationships, more creative freedom, and less doubt about who we are. This personal truth can revitalise a stale life to one of greater joy, without the fear of being thought of as 'odd' by others. Because your 'oddness' is now familiar to many, shared by many, even though still seemingly beyond the reach of some.

So, dear reader, I invite you to read *After-Death Communication* with an open mind and an open heart, allowing these pages to invoke questions and wonderings within you, as you contemplate the possibilities that communication beyond this worldly realm is not only possible, but also likely to be happening beyond our conscious awareness, all around us at all times!

Judy Guggenheim

'EVERYONE WHO SAYS THEY DON'T BELIEVE
SOMETHING THEY KNOW NOTHING ABOUT ARE NOT
ONLY FOOLS, THEY ARE IGNORANT FOOLS.'

SIR ARTHUR CONAN DOYLE

INTRODUCTION

'Insane people are always sure that they are fine. It is only the
sane people who are willing to admit that they are crazy'

NORA EPHRON

O N A BEAUTIFUL, SUNNY day in March 1981, David
Barber took his wife Margaret and nine-year-old son
Andrew to their local swimming pool, the Lido, in Droitwich.
Nestling in wooded parkland, the Lido had been referred to as an
oasis of peace. David recalls:

'As neither my wife nor I can swim, we sat at the side of
the pool, watching my son splash about. After a few
minutes, I decided to climb into the shallows and join in
the fun. Becoming more daring, I ventured further until
the water was level with my chin. Almost immediately, I
slipped, fell in slow motion and floundered helplessly on
the slippery floor. I gasped for air – but gulped only water.
'As I lay motionless, I saw a white mist at the end of
the pool. As it grew nearer, the beautiful figure of my
beloved, dead grandmother emerged from its centre,
her arms outstretched towards me. She was dressed in
a white silken gown her beautiful long hair trailing

behind her. As she grew nearer, all pain vanished. Suddenly, I was aware that my nine-year-old son had dived in to save me. He was banging my head on the floor of the pool in a vain effort to lift me. My grandmother, Amelia, was now very close and I knew that, if I turned to her, I would die. I looked at my son and knew he needed me. Immediately, the pain returned ... I felt myself rising through the water and I blacked out.

'Some years later, my son was asked if he had seen an angel under the water on that day, as I had claimed. "No," he replied, "I saw nothing ... all I know is that he's a big man and I couldn't lift him at first ... but then he rose through the water with ease, as though someone was helping me."'

I first met David when he phoned in to a radio programme which was talking about the research I was carrying out at time at the University of Birmingham. My focus and interest was on religious experiences – for my doctorate I was focusing on British people who believed they had seen or had some kind of encounter with an angel. From small beginnings the project became massive and the research and subsequent findings created a media frenzy filling the papers and was a topic debated on many a chat show, radio programme, Internet site, magazine and newspaper column. We made a BBC *Everyman* documentary around it and then came *Seeing Angels*, a book very similar to this and, indeed, the book from which this was born. It was in *Seeing Angels* that I included a sub-chapter entitled 'Granny as Your Guardian' – in it I included a few stories which had been sent to me describing seeing deceased loved ones, only the recipients had perceived them as being angels.

The words people choose to describe religious or numinous experiences is a fascinating area of discussion and something my university work particularly focused on. Language is limited to its own vocabulary, forcing people to use differing words to describe perhaps essentially the same experience – 'ghosts', 'spirits', 'guides', 'angels', 'guardian angels', 'energies' – all of these theoretically separate entities with their own description and connotations are becoming merged into one. Could we go so far as to say that all these entities are perhaps the same thing – or the same experience – just with a different label? I would suggest that for the large majority they could well be.

So, it was from such letters that my interest into ADCs was initially sparked and how the research field became incorporated into my work. It was at this time I stumbled upon Bill and Judy Guggenheim's work – The ADC Project – and I was hooked! At the time, I was doing with angel experiences what the Guggenheims were doing with accounts of ADCs – someone else was in the same boat, trying to get out to the public that such experiences, despite rarely being discussed, were incredibly common and perfectly normal. So, since 1998, Bill and Judy's book has been close beside me and I have kept up to date with their work.

As soon as *Seeing Angels* hit the shops, unsolicited testimonies came flooding in and, most interestingly, the majority grasped on to the 'Granny as Your Guardian' chapter and wrote saying they'd had exactly the same thing, outlining communications they too had had with deceased loved ones. Knowing that I had closed the cover on the angel work, I filed the letters away. To my mind, the Guggenheims had produced a thorough book on ADCs and, aside from pointing people to it, I really felt my academic and writing career was complete. So, gradually, the pile of letters grew as I returned to work in television.

However, it seemed, whichever way I turned, I always ended up back on this path. One job involved working for one of the cable channels who had asked us to cast and suggest a psychic to front a TV show which was to involve talking with the dead; another documentary involved me regaining contact with religious experience organisations and paranormal magazines, some of whom had helped me to find contributors for the angel research. A couple of these people, quite out of the blue, asked if there would be a sequel, and if not about angels then there were definitely parts that could be expanded, such as the 'Granny as Your Guardian' chapter. I laughed, thought about the growing file of letters on my shelves and shook the idea off, saying no, all that had been put to bed. And I meant it – work was great and I was loving every minute – it felt like I had finally got the angel bug out of my system and could move on ... and I was.

A couple of months later, I was asked to develop a religious series in which, as the topics were being developed it was thought one programme might include people who had experienced ADCs. Some time later I was invited to be a consultant for a documentary dealing with visions around bereavement as well as providing contacts and writing a few pieces here and there for other researchers. Throughout all this, there was still the constant dribble of more ADC letters dropping on to the doormat from readers of *Seeing Angels* all saying that, although they'd not had a vision of an angel, claimed to have seen their deceased husband or child, and wondered if this was common. The answer was yes. A definite yes.

I really felt out of my depth – as I had, indeed, done with the angel work. At the time, I felt that had almost taken me over and, even now, I am amazed at how much I and others were able to take from it. But that was a culmination of over five years' work – I knew nothing about ADCs besides scant reading, so there was no way I could develop a book from it! Yet it really felt I was being pushed back on to this path that I really hadn't anticipated treading. Rather than try to fight the tide as I had done for nigh on 12 months, I decided to simply let things be. *Que sera sera* ...

Within days, I was in talks with the publishers and, after having had a chat with Judy Guggenheim, we all agreed that there was a book here, coupled with a need for a British counterpart. A week later, I signed the contract to write the book you are now holding.

Grief and ADCs
So ADC's. One thing that has been thrown at me time and time again whilst writing this is a few totally sceptical and narrow-

minded people totally dismissing the idea – refusing to even entertain the thought of an ADC being feasible. I've had arrogant splutters of 'Why are you wasting your time with this?', 'These people are all nutters', 'ADCs aren't real, they must be some form of grief', or simply 'People don't really see their relatives when they've gone', then there is a pause followed by a more intrigued '...do they?'.

Life for every single one of us involves changes of some sort or another. From the very moment we are born, we experience change. Every move to a new home, every change in role or status, every loss of relationship, every change in beliefs and every life transition – leaving school, moving jobs, marriage, childbirth, divorce, illness or retirement – means saying goodbye to something.

Dr Elisabeth Kubler-Ross calls these changes the 'little deaths of life'. However, one of the most challenging changes that a human being can face, is the death of a loved one who helped give life meaning, purpose, safety or stability. And, of course, this affects us – big time – and we grieve.

Grief is the natural healing response to loss. Grief is not a disease to be cured, but a process all human beings experience at some time in their lives. In fact, it is the absence of grief that, in most cases, is abnormal. Grief is a journey that can be very painful, long and incredibly unpredictable. You may feel anxious, confused, sad, overwhelmed and uncertain about how to help yourself or what to do. Many grievers try to suppress or avoid their grief because it's just so painful, added to the fact our society today doesn't always support and encourage the expression of grief. The week prior to the funeral you are smothered and cocooned by friends and relations, then as soon as the last car has left the wake you are there, on your own – of course the support is still there, but those around you may be urging you to get on with your life and may be uncomfortable around your grief. So, the British stiff upper lip comes into play and we move on – just sometimes more quickly than we can cope with.

After-Death Communication and the Guggenheims

Now, closely connected to grief is the area of After-Death Communication, a term coined by Bill and Judy Guggenheim following extensive research they have carried out in America. Their assertion is that some sort of after-death communication is one of the most common spiritual experiences that we have. Indeed, a number of studies published in medical journals and other scholarly sources have established that a high percentage of bereaved people have visions of the deceased, with research showing as many as 75 per cent of grieving spouses or parents claiming to have had some sort of visitation.

Millions of bereaved people across the globe experience this type of phenomenon, which, whatever its form, helps them to deal with their loss. However, more often than not, their experience is often dismissed by family and friends as a symptom of grief or a product of the disorganisation and anxiety of the bereavement process – what is missed is their potential to heal.

Now, ADCs in other cultures are socially accepted as real communications. People who receive them are able to share them with family and friends and everyone gains from discussing these events openly. Here in the UK, it is still very different, and although taboos are slowly being broken down, the stiff upper lip prevails.

As in *Seeing Angels*, recipients to this study are from all races, religions, cultures and ages. ADCs are beyond religion, beyond philosophy and beyond culture. There are no barriers as to who experiences them – the reporting of these events transcends age, race, class, background, gender or beliefs. It is an extremely common human experience, and something which actually pulls us together as human beings is a rarity. Put simply, ADCs unite us and we need to embrace this fact.

The Guggenheims are the foremost researchers investigating this phenomenon and the first to use the word 'After-Death Communication' (ADC) in their book *Hello from Heaven!* (1996). As outlined by the Guggenheims, after-death communication is a spontaneous and direct communication from a deceased loved one. These communications do not use a psychic, medium or other third party.

According to Dr Louis LaGrand, author of *Messages and Miracles*, ADCs are not new. Cicero (106BC–43BC), a great Roman philosopher and writer, wrote essays on ADC called *On Divination*. Robert Burton (1577–1640), an English scholar, described the incidents he came across in his own times. Dr Melvin Morse, a pre-eminent Near-Death Experience researcher, says we all have the ability to communicate with loved ones after death.

In these experiences, the bereaved not only visually see the dead but may also hear, feel and sometimes even smell them. Experiences are sometimes witnessed or felt by more than one person; others convey information to the experiencer they did not previously know and could not otherwise have known.

What is an ADC?

When categorising accounts sent to them, Judy and Bill Guggenheim[2] created boundaries by which they only accepted ADC accounts into their database which were in line with the following clauses. With their permission, I have largely only included accounts into my research database of UK accounts which adhered to these following criteria:

- An After-Death Communication (ADC) is a spiritual experience that occurs when someone is contacted directly and spontaneously by a deceased family member or friend.

- An ADC is a direct experience because no intermediary or third party such as a psychic, medium or hypnotist is involved. The deceased relative or friend contacts the living person directly on a one-to-one basis.

- An ADC is a spontaneous event because the deceased loved one always initiates the contact by choosing when, where and how he or she will communicate with the living person. Since many religions and sources specifically warn against summoning 'spirits', I have excluded any letters from this research which have involved any ritual such as sèances, or those that utilised Ouija boards, crystal balls or similar devices.

All accounts which qualified were then categorised into differing types, as the chapters show. Many of these slotted neatly into the varying frames and, perhaps surprisingly, were not all visual encounters. Rather, all of our five (or perhaps this should be six?) senses were utilised:

- **Sensing** the presence of a deceased loved one – this type of experience is usually described as 'just knowing' – the experiencer just has a certain intuition that a loving presence is close by – as one lady explained to me: '... and suddenly I knew he was there. I could feel his presence. There's no way I can describe it. It was a presence I felt when he was alive, but never noticed that much. It didn't feel strange. It was very natural, like he'd never gone away.' Another wrote, 'I got a very strong sense that he was there in the kitchen with me.'

- A **Vision** of the deceased could either be seeing them in full or partially, with the clarity ranging from being a crystal-clear image to an incomplete, grainy picture.

- **Audible** experiences in which a loved one's voice is heard: 'I experienced, awake, her voice telling me gently to let my sister know that she was happy now, now that her soul is at peace.' Sometimes it is a one-way communication or, at other times, two-way, as one widow explained, 'I was thinking of nothing and trying to sleep when the radio sound faded and my husband spoke to me, his voice coming from the radio! He said, "Jenny, are you awake?" I answered and said, "Yes, I'm awake." He said, "Are you all right?" and I said, "Yes." When I realised I was talking to the radio, I was shocked, surprised and panicking to say the least ...'

The conversation can vary between being heard externally (as if someone were to talk to you right now) or internally as a sort of telepathic communication such as: 'She began to talk to me but her lips weren't moving, we could read each other's thoughts.'

- **Feeling** the deceased can range from a touch, tap, kiss, hug or caress. Someone wrote how 'suddenly, I felt two arms wrap around my waist and hug me', while another lady, on visiting her aunt's grave, '... felt her arm around my shoulders'. One lady even described her brother-in-law teasingly 'tugging' at her t-shirt.

- **Dreams**, but not normal dreams. 'The sense of awe that I experienced during the dream has stayed with me to this day ...' and people writing to me went to great lengths to describe the different nature of these dreams; usually they were incredibly vivid. They stood apart from other dreams involving their loved ones: 'I woke up. I knew it had only been a dream but at the same time I knew that it had been more than a dream and that I'd been given the chance to say goodbye.' Someone else explained after the death of her brother-in-law and young son, 'I saw them both in a dream and my brother was reaching out to hold the hands of my son as if they'd both found one another in the afterlife.'

- **Smelling** a beautiful perfume at the time of passing, be it in the presence of the dying or some time afterwards. Descriptions ranged from smelling an 'aroma of flowers at the moment our mother passed away' to someone else writing about '... a strong scent of lilies when my mother was dying, yet there weren't any flowers there'. Others smell an odour they associate with the person, be it their aftershave or brand of cigars. One lady wrote how she could '... smell Victory-V sweets from time to time and my grandmother is the only person I know who used to eat these – so I think she is still around me now'.

In most cases, people reported having one of the above experiences, although it is not uncommon for people to have them in any combination. One lady spoke of how she smelled a pot pourri-type smell seconds before her sister appeared; others have audible and visionary experiences in which all their senses are aware that someone is with them.

Other Research

Anecdotes of visions surrounding the afterlife have appeared in literature and biographies throughout the ages, but it wasn't until the twentieth century that the subject received proper scientific research. In a study, Marris[3] interviewed widows and found many spoke of feeling that their husbands were still present; about half of the sample of bereaved people Parkes saw, who required psychiatric treatment,[4] had a similar impression. Similarly, Rees reported that one in eight widows and widowers had hallucinations of hearing their dead spouse speak and a similar proportion claimed to have seen the deceased. They also referred to a general sensation of the presence of the dead person, which could continue for years, and they found it comforted them; significantly, those who had been happily married reported this more often.

After-Death Communication

Sir William Barrett, a Professor of Physics at the Royal College of Science in Dublin, was one of the first to examine the subject seriously. In 1926, he published his findings in a book entitled *Death-Bed Visions*. In the many cases he studied, he discovered some interesting aspects of the experience that are not easily explained.

It was not uncommon, for example, for the dying people who saw these visions to identify friends and relatives whom they thought were still living. But in each case, according to Barrett, it was later discovered that these people actually were dead. (Remember, communication then wasn't what it is today, and it might take weeks or even months to learn that a friend or loved one had died.)

Barrett found it curious that children quite often expressed surprise that the 'angels' they saw in their dying moments did not have wings. If the death-bed vision is just an hallucination, wouldn't a child see an angel as it is most often depicted in art and literature – with large, white wings?

More extensive research into these mysterious visions went on in the 1960s and '70s by Dr Karlis Osis of the American Society for Psychical Research. In this research, and for a book he published in 1977 entitled *At the Hour of Death*, Osis considered thousands of case studies and interviewed more than 1,000 doctors, nurses and others who attended the dying. The work uncovered a number of fascinating consistencies:

- Although some dying people report seeing angels and other religious figures (and sometimes even mythical figures), the vast majority claim to see familiar people who had previously passed away.

- Very often, the friends and relatives seen in these visions express directly that they have come to help take them away.

- The dying person is reassured by the experience and expresses great happiness with the vision. Contrast this with the confusion or fear that a non-dying person would experience at seeing a 'ghost'. The dying also seem quite willing to go with these apparitions.

- The dying person's mood – even state of health – seems to change. During these visions, a once depressed or pain-ridden person is overcome with elation and momentarily relieved of pain ... until death strikes.

- These experiencers do not seem to be hallucinating or to be in an altered state of consciousness; rather, they appear to be quite aware of their real surroundings and conditions.

- Whether or not the dying person believes in an afterlife is irrelevant; the experience and reactions are the same.[5]

At the precise moment of death and the accompanying experiences of late relatives and past loved ones appearing to lead the dying to the next realm, relatively little systematic work has been done on actual post-mortem visitations to the living.[6] Cleiren's Leiden Study[7] showed that, 14 months after a death, about a third of the bereaved people studied felt a sense of presence of the dead and also 'talked' to the dead, either vocally or in a silent inner 'conversation'. Studies suggest that as many as 66 per cent of widows experience apparitions of their departed husbands[8] and, in addition, Finucane's historical analysis of the way in which the ghostly dead appear to the living illustrates the point that, up to the eighteenth century, ghosts adopted a normal vocal quality, while by the twentieth century they tend to be mute.[9] This ties in well with the experiences reported to me – in only one did a deceased relative speak. However, in some accounts, an angel accompanied the deceased speaking on their behalf, assuring all would be well.

The universal experience of apparitions has found its way into the language and folklore of cultures all over the world, from a time long before the beginning of recorded history. Indeed, the storyline of *Hamlet*, one of Shakespeare's greatest plays, was based around an ADC, as it is in *A Christmas Carol* where Ebenezer Scrooge's deceased business partner, Jacob Marley, returns to warn him of his fate if he refuses to change his materialistic values and become more charitable. Although disbelieving at first, Scrooge eventually takes heed of the warning. Then, of course, there are accounts in the Bible and, although somewhat different to those of ordinary human beings, there are the various appearances Jesus made and visions of the Blessed Virgin Mary are recorded throughout Catholic literature.

Increasing Belief in the Afterlife

Interestingly, one of the most authoritative spokesmen of the Roman Catholic Church recently raised eyebrows among the faithful by declaring that the Church does now, in fact, believe in the feasibility of communication with the dead.[10] The Rev Gino Concetti, chief theological commentator for the Vatican newspaper, *L'Osservatore Romano*, denied he was signalling any change in approach, but agreed that his remarks might come as a surprise to many believers. He said the Church remained opposed to the raising of spirits, but added, 'Communication is possible between those who live on this earth and those who live in a state of eternal repose, in heaven or purgatory. It may even be that God lets our loved ones send us messages to guide us at certain moments in our life.' He went on to suggest that dead relatives could be responsible for prompting impulses and triggering inspiration – and even for 'sensory manifestations', such as appearances in dreams.

It is also interesting to look at how beliefs are changing. Professor

Michael Earl[11] for example says one might think, amid this socio-cultural evolution, that there would be a decreasing belief in and concern with personal immortality. Like the concerns with demons and witches which used to perturb ancient (and perhaps not so ancient) man, we should by now have grown out of this fixation. But we have not. If anything – and whether it is because we are entering a new spiritual era or not – people are communicating belief in an afterlife and subsequent experiences more and more.

Indeed, for its 1984, 1988, 1989 and 1991 *General Social Surveys*, NORC[12] included the question: 'How often have you felt as though you were really in touch with someone who had died?'

Below is the breakdown of responses:

RESPONSE	FREQUENCY	% OF TOTAL
NEVER	3057	58%
1 OR 2 TIMES	1201	22.8%
SEVERAL TIMES	565	10.7%
OFTEN	245	4.6%
CAN'T ANSWER	202	3.8%
TOTAL	5,270	100%

A massive survey was carried out and has since been updated – again, this was to assess belief in the afterlife. Surprisingly, in the update to this study, over 39,000 individuals from 32 countries were surveyed. Belief in the afterlife in many countries, Great Britain included, has definitely increased since the 1991 survey.

Questions

Over a considerable period of time, I have wrestled with the whole idea of the afterlife and After-Death Communication – a great deal of conversation has ensued and still, like many, I am none the wiser. Having a background and degrees at whatever level in theology and anthropology doesn't necessarily bring you any closer to the answer – if there is one.

Admittedly, there have been times when I thought that this book would never materialise, be it due to events in my own life or indeed external happenings such as worrying about categorising and distributing accounts into the varying chapters and so forth, but whenever doubt crept in, something always happened to banish it, be it a new letter dropping onto the doormat which made all the hairs on the back of my neck stand on end, or commitments falling through so I could take a much needed fortnight off to concentrate solely on writing. I am a true believer in everything happening for a reason and, despite the times I thought perhaps this book wasn't meant to be, it seemingly *was* meant, as it all came together with such ease.

Some days as I sat typing up these accounts, I became totally detached from the whole idea – disillusioned even. With the basic medical knowledge that I have, I can piece together some of the evidence and guess that such and such a person's ADC was stress-induced, another's was willed, this person was suffering a known hallucinatory illness, this person admits to being on morphine at the time, but this person said it was a dream, so how can it be different? Can one really reach another plane in a dream state? Each night, I dream of my family, friends or neighbours, but they don't know what I have dreamt or where we went or what we did. I didn't physically meet up with them and go to the places in the dream – why should these ADC dreams be any different? Well, hardly an argument to peg your hat on, but they are different simply because they stand out, as Alison Myers explains, 'Whilst listening to Radio 2 on my way home from work a couple of months ago, I heard an interview in which you talked about your book on angels and your latest research into communication with deceased relatives or friends through vivid dreams. You said that anyone who had had such a dream would know what you were talking about, and I believe I do.'

Now, who am I to assess the authenticity of these accounts? Who am I to sit back and determine the causing factors? It is all too easy to dismiss paranormal occurrences – it is far harder to open your mind and say, 'I don't know.' And I really do *not* know. All I know is that every person who has written to me on this matter writes with an intense conviction – 95 per cent of the cases were single, one-off isolated communications or visions – and something which will always remain with them. They provide an enormous sense of comfort, or guidance and relief that loved ones are OK.

Some people themselves trivialise or dismiss the experiences as 'Oh, I was imagining it ... seeing what I wanted to see', and putting it down to a grief-induced hallucination of some sort or other. What they are not doing is seeing these communications (whether their origin be created by the brain or something greater) as being hugely constructive and positive. By missing out on this, they therefore cut themselves off from their potential to heal.

However, as with most types of religious experience, scientists will try to explain them as being the result of extreme emotion. However, I argue the case otherwise. As the accounts I have collected here show, some ADC experiences may occur prior to the recipient knowing about the death of the person who appears to them. This observation, along with numerous documented ADCs which have occurred ten or more years hence from the time of death of the loved one, thoroughly refutes the argument that ADCs are only acute grief-related reactions. How on earth can someone be in a state of grief when they not only do not know, but are not even anticipating this person's sudden death?

Something else which annoys me about religious and numinous experiences is the taboo which still exists today. Slowly, people are more accepting, and I am greeted with less scowls and suspicion. People are wary of the unknown and many are unable to discuss personal experiences for fear of ridicule. After explaining an incredible experience of seeing her husband some months after he suddenly passed over one lady told how '... when I told my best friend the next day what I saw, she thought I was going mad. I was very insulted.' Sadly, as with other taboos still prevalent even in the twenty-first century, such experiences are difficult to divulge. But why, if one in three of us have them? For fear of ridicule, for fear of being told you simply imagined or dreamt it — but as you will see in the following pages, to the people who experienced these visitations, they were like nothing else. They are as vivid today as they were at the time — and for some that was 30, 40 and, to one man, over 50 years ago.

Truth v Reality

What the people contributing to these pages share is something intensely memorable and poignant — they don't care whether the experience was 'real' or subconsciously 'induced' ... all that matters is that it happened and carried a huge amount of significance and meaning to that individual. And so we enter the debate of truth versus reality. The 'truth' behind it all is irrelevant — it is the reality of the experience that I am concerned with. Even now, in the twenty-first century, nearly all the letters began with justifications and testimonies of the author's sanity, integrity and honesty. We are unable here simply to state, 'I had an experience the other day which involved ...' Most people would laugh, scoff or try to rationalise it. I think we need to ask ourselves why this is the case. Is it to quell our hidden fears of the unknown?

Pam James, went to great lengths in her letter to describe herself as an 'ordinary person who has questioned life after death for about ten years now ... I speak the absolute truth and hope you will believe what happened as I have no reason to fabricate any of this.'

Others articulated similar sentiments:

> 'I'm not a fruitcake, but what the death of my husband has taught me is that death is not final and that there are things that we cannot understand or even begin to explain in any rational way — we just have to accept them.'
> (Kate Boydell)

> 'I do hope you believe me. I know it happened. I was not expecting it and I treasure the memory of it.'
> (Marc Oxley)

'I am a logical person of sound mind and it still baffles me as to why? How? And especially, why me?'
(Collette Donoghue)

'One reason for me writing to you is the possibility that this has happened to someone else. In this case, I will be greatly interested and much consoled that I am not mad, nor imagining things as part of my bereavement. This is certainly not the case, it has been an experience that has altered my outlook on life, death and the afterlife ...'
(Isabel)

Why is it people are so afraid and reluctant to share such an important happening in their life? Why can't we, in today's society, freely discuss such phenomena? Why isn't this topic being widely studied and investigated as potential evidence for life after death? Wouldn't they fulfil the promises of the world's great religions that we will all survive physical death and be reunited with our loved ones?

I want to end here with the final paragraph of the letter I received from Mary Malcolmson: 'Well, for what they are worth, those are my experiences, maybe not much, I know, to someone else, but to me they changed my life.'

And life-changing they are. Not all of these accounts are dramatic; seeing your granny or father at the foot of the bed, although a powerful and dramatic experience to the recipient, is not necessarily so for the reader!

So, Mary's sentence is really the essence of the book – the weight of evidence for both sides of the argument is pretty balanced, favouring neither believers in ADCs nor non-believers. The range of experiences simply speak for themselves, and it has always been my intention that this should be a book for the general public by the general public. I am not trying to prove nor disprove any authenticity or probability – that is up to you.

1

THE POINT OF DEATH

'It is only with the heart that one can see rightly.
What is essential is invisible to the eye'

ANTOINE DE SAINT EXURPERY,
LE PETIT PRINCE

Death-Bed Visions

A DEATH-BED VISION IS a powerful, comforting experience the dying and their family members often encounter just before death occurs. The dying will often report visions of angels, deceased loved ones or religious figures, moments, hours, days or even weeks before their actual death takes place. Generally speaking, these visions tend to lessen the fear of dying and make the passing an easier transition for all concerned.

Sceptics and, indeed, family members who are not familiar with the death-bed vision phenomenon will often ask, 'Couldn't these "visions" just be the by-product of a dying brain?' In the 1920s, 1960s and '70s, several researchers asked this specific question and decided to put the phenomenon to the test. What they discovered was astounding – visions experienced by the dying were most often of deceased relatives. During the vision, deceased relatives would appear to the dying person to offer support, guidance and assistance as death drew near. Interestingly, in some death-bed vision accounts, the dying individual received visitations from relatives they did not know were already deceased. While scientifically investigating this phenomenon, they also discovered that these departing visions have been reported by the dying for centuries. Even President Abraham Lincoln had a death-bed vision, just before his own assassination.[13]

Death-bed visions are not just the stuff of stories and movies. They are incredibly common and surprisingly similar across nationalities, religions and cultures. Instances of these unexplained visions have been recorded throughout history and stand as one of the most compelling proofs of life after death.

Apparitions of deceased friends and loved ones have been reported to appear to escort the dying to the other side. In turn, the dying appear to loved ones here right at, or moments before, their departing to say goodbye. It is a phenomenon that is more common than you might imagine, and there is a significant similarity with accounts from the chapters 'Angels of Mercy' and 'Angels of Death' in *Seeing Angels* where deceased relatives often appeared with an angel in tow to escort the dying to the next dimension.

'Father lies dying. The hospital is quiet. Visiting hours are over and the sun has long since set. Father has been sleeping off and on all day. His doctor says the end could come at any time. His wrinkled, sunken eyes open slowly. His breathing has been laboured, but now it seems to ease and soften. His eyes track to a corner of the room where there is only a faded green vinyl chair. Father smiles.

' "You're here," he whispers.

'His daughter, determined to be with him in his final moments, takes his hand. "Yes, I'm here, Dad," she says. But she knows he's not looking at her.

' "No," Father says, never taking his eyes off the corner of the room. "There. It's your uncle Jerome. I never thought I'd see him again."

'The daughter glances to the corner but, of course, sees nothing. Father seems coherent. In fact, she hasn't seen him so alert in days.

' "Oh my!" Father's smile broadens. "And Lucille! And mother is with them! They ... they say they have come to help me. They have come to take me with them. Can't you see them? They look so wonderful!"

'The daughter wraps her father's hand in both of hers. She doesn't know what to think. Father closes his eyes again and the smile slowly fades from his lips. He releases one long, last breath ... and is gone.'

A similar scenario was told by Veronica Mooney who described her father when seriously ill, dying of lung cancer: '... he could not do anything except lie on the bed – he was too weak. He used to reach his arms out as if someone was there and say, "Eileen" (his late sister) and sometimes say, "Mum", he also said, "Millie", (which was his mother-in-law who had also passed away).'

Connie Jones described a similar occurrence that happened in 1953 when she was sitting with her father:

'He had been bed-bound for three months with bronchitis, he was totally lucid and was in pain with gangrene (which we now know was from undiagnosed diabetes). Two days before he died, he was sitting up in bed and I witnessed him talking directly to someone – only there was no one there. He said, "Fred, I'm coming, I'm coming, Fred, wait for me." Fred was his eldest son who had committed suicide in 1931.'

Among all the letters I received, doctors, nurses, hospice workers and carers featured strongly with testimonies. Joanie Spiegel explains:

'Working [at the] hospice, it is truly a privilege to sit

with someone as they approach the end of their life. There was one night in the hospice where a lady was struggling for breath; having lung cancer, it must be one of the most frightening ways to die. As I sat with her, I felt a presence at the foot of her bed. Slowly, a young girl of about seven years gradually emerged wearing a lovely pink frock. She gazed at the lady with such love ... also, to the back of the bed appeared two angels with huge wings ... they were waiting to guide her on her journey. The lady suddenly opened her eyes and, as she saw the girl, a calmness enveloped her. She then took her last breath. After such a long, hard struggle with her disease, there was peace all around. It transpired unknown to me that she had lost a daughter aged seven and never got over it. It seemed a great healing process had occurred in that moment.'

Similarly, Joy Snell grew up in Ireland before becoming a nurse in England. She had an extraordinary series of spiritual experiences which she recounts in her book, *The Ministry Of Angels* whereby she was frequently at the bedside of a dying patient and saw the deceased family members and friends who came to assist their loved one in making his or her transition. Joy also describes many out-of-body ADCs she had with her mother, father, brother and others.

Ray Grindell's experience describes the reaction of an animal at the moment of death and, although different, I think it ties in well:

'I was 16 and living with my parents and widowed grandmother ... my grandfather George had died a few years earlier. My grandmother became critically ill and was being nursed by my mother in an upstairs bedroom. My mother would sit at the bedside of my grandmother with our pet dog, Blackie, a cocker spaniel, for company. I must stress that Blackie was absolutely fearless, be it of humans or other animals.

'On this particular evening, my father and I were sitting downstairs in the lounge listening to the radio when we heard something rushing down the stairs whining and howling. As we opened the door, Blackie rushed in with all the hair standing up on his back, and he rushed under the table, whining and cowering, and was absolutely petrified. My father then called out to my mother who was still upstairs and she then related what had happened.

'As she was sitting at the bedside, my grandmother came out of the coma she was in, lifted her head from the pillow and, without any sign of illness, gave a brilliant smile, looked up to the corner of the room and said, "Hello, George," and at that second passed away. At the same second, Blackie who was laid at my mother's feet, shot up and looked in the exact place where my grandmother had looked and, with absolute terror and hair on end, whining, shot out of the room and flew down the stairs to my father and I.

'I am convinced that both my grandmother and Blackie had seen an angel that had come down for my grandmother in the guise of my grandfather.'

Accounts like Ray's of the dying reaching out to others unseen to us are commonplace. Carol Ann Marsh, for example, was in hospital recovering from an operation when she observed an elderly lady who had been brought on to the ward with a blood clot in her leg:

'Her very serious condition meant that the nurses had to constantly treat her. Throughout the second night, she kept raising herself up, arms outstretched towards the bottom of her bed then shaking her head and sinking back down in great pain. As she was keeping myself and, indeed, the whole ward awake, I was watching her throughout that night and wondering if she was being "called", but fighting for her life here. In the morning, the screens were put around her and she had passed away.'

The following account was from a palliative care nurse who had been working alongside a couple, who, for the sake of confidentiality, we shall call Mr and Mrs A. Mr A had been admitted to hospital after being diagnosed with an incurable disease. The doctors were optimistic that treatment may slow down the progress of the disease and improve his symptoms, so the nurse had a lot of contact over the next few weeks with Mr and Mrs A, both by telephone and in the outpatients' department.

'At the beginning of [November], Mr A became acutely ill at home and was taken to the A & E department with a condition unrelated to his previous diagnosis. He was admitted to hospital and, despite active treatment, his condition deteriorated over the next few days and I was heavily involved in advising about his symptom management and providing psychological support for the family.

'On the morning of [his death], I had a message to say that Mr A had just died; he had been comfortable and his family had been at his bedside. The family were still on the ward and asked if I could go down and see them, which I did.

'I left the ward at the same time as the trolley taking Mr A's body to the mortuary. I held the doors open to let the porters take the trolley through, and I followed them down the corridor until they stopped at the lifts. As I walked past, I brushed my hand lightly against the side of the trolley and thought, Goodbye, Mr A, and continued walking towards the stairs.

'Next to the lifts is a stairwell that staff generally use, rather than waste time waiting for the lifts. It is always busy and, even if you don't see anyone, you can usually hear doors banging, people chatting, bleeps, etc. The building has seven floors, and I entered the stairwell on the third floor to go to the wards on the sixth floor.

'As I went through the doors, I noted it was very quiet with none of the usual hustle and bustle. My thoughts turned away completely to a situation totally unrelated to work that was worrying me ... I can remember *exactly* what I was thinking about. Suddenly, I became aware of a feeling of stillness, with no sense of time, sound or space and everything seemed both incredibly intense but also very nebulous ...

'As I became more aware of these feelings, I felt that I was contained in a beam of clear, white light that went the whole height and almost the whole width of the building. Then I *sensed*, rather than saw, a pair of enormous wings coming around from the back of the beam of light, completely enfolding me and I *knew* it was an angelic being. I was overwhelmed with emotion and an amazing sense of safety, protection, love and compassion, and I felt both very calm and yet incredibly elated.

'And then, as soon as I tried to focus on what was happening, it was gone as quickly as it had come. I suddenly felt myself being dragged back ... I felt dense and heavy, could hear noises and felt temperature. My overriding feeling at that stage was that, for however long it was, time had stood still, almost as if I'd stepped into another dimension to have this experience.

'Later, when I had time to think about this experience, I wasn't really able to make any more of it, other than I know it did happen ... I've been up and down those same stairs every working day since then, without a hint of any sensations or experiences.'

Unprompted Appearances of the Deceased

Here is the first strong evidence that can potentially disprove the idea that all after-death communications are grief-induced hallucinations – how can one be going through the first stages of bereavement when one isn't even aware that the death has occurred? This very occurrence happened to a friend who had a brother who'd been in a car crash and was on life support for weeks. One night she 'saw' him come into her bedroom and say, 'I'm OK, Sis.' It was only the next day that she was told that the machine had been turned off at the same time she had had the dream. Similarly, Pauline Audoir had her paternal grandmother appear to her at a friend's house and sat opposite her. 'It was some hours later that my father informed me she'd passed at the time she appeared.'

Such visions and communications have appeared to a huge variety of people throughout history. Anatole France tells how his great-aunt saw a mirror vision of Robespierre dying at approximately the same time he was shot in the jaw:

'On the night of 27 July 1794, she was looking in a mirror when she shouted, "I see him! I see him! How pale he is! Blood is flowing from his mouth! His teeth and jaws are shattered! God be praised. The bloodthirsty wretch will drink no more blood but his own." Then she cried out and fainted.'

Karen Browne, in 1998, recalls the time her beloved grandfather passed away:

'I was sound asleep lying very snug and warm in my bed when, all of a sudden, I became wide awake. For absolutely no reason, I woke suddenly from my deep sleep. I sat up in bed and saw my grandfather standing at the side of my bed. He was smiling at me and his gaze was radiating pure love. Then he spoke using his pet name for me saying, "I'm going away now, my wee dove." I smiled back at him and lay back down to sleep, pausing only to look at the clock before closing my eyes. The time was 6.00am. Good, I thought, I don't have to get up for work for another hour or so, and with that I resumed my deep and peaceful sleep.

'My Nana and Papa (Mum's parents) lived in the small ground-floor flat below us and we were extremely close. For some reason, I did not feel the need to question why Papa had been in my room at that time in the morning or to ask where he was going. Bizarrely I just felt that it was the most natural thing in the world to see my grandfather standing at the side of my bed at 6.00am!

'I was in a peaceful dreamless sleep aware of nothing else until I heard a blood-chilling scream followed by the phone ringing in our hall. I jumped out of bed and lifted the receiver to hear my Nan's voice sobbing for me to come quick, that she thought my Papa was dead. I felt sick with shock and, by this time, my parents and younger brother were in the hall, too. "Please, God, no," I prayed, "please not my Papa." Everyone rushed downstairs except me. I could not bear to see my beloved Papa lying dead in his bed. I stayed in my room for some time trying to will him back to life, until finally I knew I had to face the truth and went downstairs.

'Everyone was in shock – my poor wee Nana was heartbroken; she had been with my Papa since she was 16 and had borne him seven children – four daughters and three sons. It was a large and happy family and everyone adored my Nana and Papa. I was the eldest of

21 grandchildren and, as is common of many first grandchildren, I had always had a special place in my Nana and Papa's affections.

'One would think under the circumstances I would be devastated, but somehow I felt strangely calm and almost detached from the situation. I called the family GP and also our priest and went about the unenviable task of telephoning the rest of the family with the awful news. Soon the small flat was bursting at the seams with family members all in shock and heartbroken. I, however, remained calm and even took some of the younger grandchildren out shopping for food supplies for all our visitors whilst the awful necessities of dealing with a death, such as the visit from the undertakers, went ahead.

'My beloved Papa was prepared and laid out in his coffin in his bedroom whilst family and friends came to weep and pay homage. I still did not want to see the body but felt I should as my mother wanted me to pay my respects. I went into the room alone and looked at the figure in the coffin and realised it was just a shell lying there and that my Papa had indeed gone away. It was then that what had happened earlier that morning hit me. My Papa had come to say goodbye. I felt strangely comforted and felt sure that there must be a life after death. I also felt a sense of irony as my Papa was very much against ghosts and anything supernatural yet he had said goodbye to me on his passing. I felt privileged, but also guilty, as I did not grieve for him as everyone else did – I knew he was dead but not gone.

'Some time after the funeral, I decided to look at my Papa's death certificate as I was not certain as to the actual cause of death. He had died peacefully in his sleep of a massive heart-attack and the time of the death was estimated at 6.00am – exactly the time he had appeared to me to say goodbye.'

Following a distinguished career in publishing, including President of Prentice-Hall International, Kenneth T. Hurst relates a full appearance by his mother in his book, *Live Life First Class!*. She came to him looking as she had in her youth, wearing clothes of the 1920s. His mother stood next to his bed and beamed a lovely radiant smile at him. The next morning, he learned by phone that she had died in England at the exact time she appeared to him in America.

When Mrs Collins was 16 or 17 years old, she went to the local cinema with a friend:

> 'On the right-hand-side wall, there was a large clock lit with red and green bulbs. You couldn't miss it. I was sitting enjoying the film – Shirley Temple was in it. Perhaps you have never heard of her; but in those days, she was a beautiful little child star. Anyway, the cinema was crowded, the sweet papers were rattling, and the monkey nut shells on the floor were crackling as they got trod on. Shirley Temple was on top of a baby grand piano tap-dancing to the music, when suddenly everything was obliterated from me. I couldn't hear anything, I couldn't see anything, I wasn't aware of any other people around me; the clock I spoke about earlier had also gone.
>
> 'I must have still been looking ahead of me at what had been the film, but now it was also pitch-black. Then my little cousin's face came on the right-hand side where the screen had been. She was smiling at me. I still don't know how long it lasted, it seemed an eternity, but as suddenly as it came, it went. Everything was back to normal. I was seeing and hearing the film, the people, monkey nut shells, everything. I looked up at the clock – eight o'clock it said. The film finished.
>
> 'My friend had a habit of walking part way home with me from the cinema. I didn't say a word to her

about what I had seen although I kept thinking about it. We had gone quite a long way up the road, when from another direction Grace (my friend) was called. It was an older sister calling her. Grace went to see what she wanted, but I remained where I was. I knew, though, what it was about; Grace's family lived quite close to where my cousin, whom I had "seen" in the cinema, lived. When she came back to me, we set off walking again but Grace wasn't speaking, so I said to her, "What's the matter?" "Oh nothing," she said. Still no conversation. So I said outright, "Is it Beryl (my cousin)?" She looked alarmed, started spluttering and said, "Well, yes." Still no more; so I said, "Is she dead?" With that she looked at me as though I had grown horns; more spluttering, then she said again, "Well, yes." I asked what time she'd died. "Around 8.00pm," she said. I replied, "Yes, it was 8.00pm on the cinema clock."

'At the moment she had died, Beryl had shown herself to me on her way to the ethereal world. She was only nine years old, and had had a most dreadful end, they told me, when I arrived home. She used to call me "Nin" and we were very fond of each other. I had seen her a few days before and she showed me a little dress she had made for her doll. She was so proud of it. She had died with congestion of the lungs.'

Remote ADCs

The following accounts all share the fact that the recipient was away (some on different continents) from the dying at the time of their death, yet had some kind of experience at that same precise moment they took their last breath.

Barbara Waller's father was admitted to hospital with Parkinson's Disease when she was just two years old, and he stayed there from then on:

'When I was 15 or thereabouts, I arrived home one evening at six o'clock (I heard it announced on a neighbour's radio). Our dog was waiting and, as I walked in our front door, I saw coming down our stairs a man with a dark coat or cloth around him and a white face but his eyes were happy looking. Our usually aggressive dog let out a howl and ran into the front room with all his hackles up – I took one last look at this man only to see him disappear as I watched frightened. I ran and joined the dog behind the chair in the front room.

'A few minutes later, my mother arrived home. She pooh-poohed my experience and said I was imagining things, but at about half-past six came a knock on our front door (no phones in those days) and there stood a policeman, who said, "I'm sorry, Mrs Burbage, but I have to tell you that your husband died at six o'clock tonight." My dad just came to say goodbye, I guess – oh, and by the way, I'm 71 years old now ...'

Eight years ago, Catherine Conaty lost her father to cancer:

'It was a very swift loss and he had only been diagnosed a month before his death. As you can imagine, it was a huge shock – I had been especially close to him. It was lung cancer which had spread to his brain. As he had always been particularly clever, this seemed a very cruel way for him to go.

'Four years prior to my father's death, I had lost my brother to the same disease (he died aged only 38). Again, just like Dad's cancer, it went undiagnosed until practically the end. I was very close to my brother, especially as a child. My father had been absolutely devastated by my brother's sudden death and I don't think ever got over it.

'As I said previously, we as a family were taken completely by surprise when Dad was diagnosed and, at the time, the doctors gave him six months to live. Of course, you never know when someone with a terminal illness is likely to die, but we weren't prepared for it to happen quite so suddenly.

'On the evening of 10 August 1994, I went to bed at my usual time. I had seen my father that day during the morning and had witnessed him trying to complete a crossword. He was not eating very much and was obviously very ill, but we had a short conversation and he smiled at me as I left the bedroom ...

'I remember definitely going to sleep but then waking very suddenly with an absolute certainty that someone or something was in the room with me. It was a definite "feeling". I remember struggling to open my eyes and, on doing so, I was conscious of something "dark" right in front of me. The bedroom was dark but not pitch-black as we have a street light right outside our window. Within a matter of seconds, I felt something or someone touch me lightly on the head. I was initially terrified and remember trying to get up out of bed but finding I just couldn't move. The touching went on and I remember feeling strangely comforted. I then heard a voice say to me, "Don't worry, you will be all right." I then remember sensing that I knew the person speaking to me but I couldn't quite place them. It must have been seconds later that I was able to move again and I remember looking at the clock on the bedside table. It was 3.00am on 12 August, which just happened to be my wedding anniversary.

'At 6.00am that morning, after returning to sleep, I learned of my father's death. At once, I felt a strange sense of peace as I remembered the "visitor" in the night. I had the most utter conviction that the person in the room that night had been my brother. I knew then that the "blackness" I had witnessed in front of me had been his legs – he always wore black trousers in life – I really don't remember him wearing anything other than black!

'I was later told that my father died somewhere around 3.00am. Everything seemed to fit together and I had the overwhelming feeling that my brother had "come to collect" my father so that he would be safe in passing over.

'I am not a deeply religious person and am not a believer of the supernatural, but I do have an open mind and I know what I witnessed that night was not a dream. It has stayed with me all these years and even now, just conveying the story, makes it seem so real.'

Now, not all people reported actually seeing the deceased as such at the time of their death. For some it was a dramatic rush of wind seemingly coming from nowhere, or light filled the room, or perhaps it was a feeling that something had happened, or they simply witnessed something that, at the time, was inexplicable.

Wind
In 1967, Brenda and her husband lived in Devon. The husband of a couple who were friends of theirs went to stay with them for a few months while starting a job in Devon before their new bungalow was finished. Brenda takes up the story eight years later:

'By then my husband had become mentally ill and one day, feeling depressed, he had taken an overdose of tablets. I had come back from shopping to find him in a deep sleep and telephoned for an ambulance. I couldn't go with him to hospital because I had to fetch the children home from school. As we arrived home, a neighbour called to ask if there was a problem as she had seen the ambulance. As we couldn't talk then, she promised to call around later.

'Later that evening, when the children were in bed, I was sitting in my dining room which was at the rear of the house when there was a loud, sharp "rat-a-tat-tat" on either the window or door at the back of the house. Thinking it was my neighbour, I hurried to the back door but there was nobody there. I also realised that no one could get round the back as the side gate was too high and was locked. I sat down again only for the same thing to happen a few minutes later. Again, there was nobody there.

'By this time, I was getting worried and phoned the hospital again only to be told my husband was all right. I sat down again and, a few minutes later, a gust of wind rushed through the room and blew my skirt up, although there were no doors or windows open.

'I worried about this for a few days and made gentle enquiries around to see if anyone had died, but couldn't find anyone and gradually forgot about it. About six months later, I received a letter from some more friends in Devon who informed me that the friend who had been a lodger with us had died on the exact same date the strange things happened.'

A similar wind-type experience happened when Frederick Pine was a bachelor working in Singapore. He had quite an active social life with frequent invitations out, especially in the evenings – cocktail parties and dinners and so forth. His invitation for the evening in question was unusual in that it was from a relative – his nephew – at that time a Lieutenant-Commander in the Royal Navy, stationed at the Singapore Naval Base. As he usually did when invited out, he had told his Chinese housekeeper at breakfast that no dinner would be required when he returned home that evening. As usual, he was made a pot of tea, and when she came to collect the tea things, she asked if she could go shopping:

'This was a most unusual request and the only time she made it in the ten or more years she worked for me. Apart from that, there were other reasons why her one-off desire to go out evening shopping surprised me and, in view of the connection I am bound to make between this and subsequent events, it would be appropriate to give them.

'Firstly, if she wished to go out shopping, there was plenty of time for her to do so during the day when I was away at work. She also had time off each weekend from Saturday afternoon to Sunday evening, which she spent with other *amah*s in downtown Singapore. There was never any need for her to go out shopping for food or other household items. I was a customer of a Chinese merchant who was able to supply anything a household was likely to require, and all my *amah* did was to ring up and give her order. This was delivered promptly to the door and I was sent a monthly account.

'Finally, the house was in an upmarket area of Singapore and there were no shops in the vicinity, the nearest being quite a walk away. My *amah* was an elderly lady of quite a nervous disposition and I would not have expected her to go wandering about on quiet, lonely roads in the dark. However, I said, "Of course, go right ahead," and thought no more of it at the time. She disappeared to her own rooms at the back of the house and, after a while, I went upstairs, had a shower and put on a suit.

'When I came downstairs again, I looked at my watch and saw that it was a quarter-to-seven. My invitation had been for seven-thirty and, as it was only a half-hour drive to the Naval Base, I decided that I had better use up some time to avoid arriving early. I sat down in my usual easy chair and, as it was getting dark, switched on the standard lamp. Singapore houses tend to be built on quite spacious lines and this house had a good-sized reception area which communicated through an archway to the dining room. From where I was sitting, I could see part of the dining room through the archway. I lit a cigarette and started to look through the *Singapore Straits Times*.

'Suddenly, a loud noise started in the dining room – the best way that I can describe it is that it sounded like a rushing of wind. Outside the house, it was the usual calm, tropical evening. This rushing noise then travelled out through the archway and, quite slowly, across the room until it was above my head. Suddenly, it stopped and two loud bangs like pistol shots appeared to come from the ceiling. I was completely taken aback by this and, although in hindsight it seemed silly, the only thing I could think of by way of an explanation was that, while I had been upstairs changing and the *amah* had gone out, a burglar had got in.

'I rushed around the house, upstairs and downstairs, but found nothing, and then got into my car and drove to the Naval Base. During the evening, I said nothing to my nephew about the occurrence in the house. This was out of character for me; normally I would have wanted to discuss such a strange event with the first person I met after it. I do not know why I said nothing, but my silence was certainly not the result of a conscious decision on my part.

'I got back home around midnight and went to bed. About six-thirty in the morning, there was a knock at my bedroom door. When I opened it, my *amah* was standing there and she handed me a cablegram. It was from my sister in Plymouth to say that my mother had died. This came as a considerable shock to me; although my mother had been poorly with heart trouble, I had not expected her death. Also, and perhaps because I was the youngest, I had a closer relationship with my mother than either my brother or sister, even through much of my adult life had been spent working away from home and overseas.

'During the two days it took to arrange a flight to the UK for the funeral, I said nothing to my office colleagues about the occurrence in my house, although I had already connected it to my mother's death. Here, again, there was no conscious decision on my part not to mention it.

'When I arrived in London, I got a train to Plymouth and my brother met me at the station. I said to him, "What time of the day did she die? Was it about half-past twelve in the afternoon?" He looked surprised and replied, "Yes, how did you know?" I said, "That was 7.00pm Singapore time, and she called on me then."

'The Singapore time zone has since been changed to eight hours ahead of GMT, but then it was seven-and-a-half hours ahead. With British Summer Time in operation, the actual time difference was six-and-a-half hours so that 12.30pm GMT was 7.00pm Singapore time.

'As far as I am concerned, I accept this experience as proof that some part of the human entity survives the physical death of the body and that it can transcend space and time. My mother had never been east of Suez in her life, but she knew where to find me.

'There is also the one-off absence from the house of my *amah* on that weekday evening. I cannot accept this as being merely coincidental, especially having regard to the attendant circumstances which I have described. If coincidence is ruled out, it seems to me that there can only be one alternative conclusion. This is that, in advance of her death, my mother was able to put the idea into my *amah's* mind that she should go out shopping and so get her out of the house. I have concluded that my mother was able to "stage-manage" the whole affair and have me sitting quietly and alone at the time of her death.'

Light

David Redknap's mother was brought up in South Africa from the age of four and met his father when he came out to South Africa from England during the Second World War. She moved to England with him around 1945:

'In about 1958, as my mother was drifting off to sleep in her bedroom one night, she became aware of a blue light hovering in the bedroom. She distinctly heard the words, "It's all right now, everything is as it should be." She felt a sense of peace when this happened. Mum's sister would write on a regular basis, and when the next letter arrived, it carried the news of Mum's mother's passing.'

Similarly, Mrs Wyborn's mother had been dreadfully crippled with rheumatoid arthritis and had been confined to a wheelchair for her last 20 years. Towards the end of her life, she also developed cancer. Eventually, it was clear that her strength was ebbing fast, but no one could be sure just how long she would live. Mrs Wyborn and her husband lived over 100 miles away and had been planning on visiting her one weekend but a severe migraine attack put a stop to the visit. Two nights later, Mrs Wyborn awoke at 1.00am and saw a very bright light at the foot of the bed and experienced 'a feeling of inexplicable happiness and wellbeing'. She then fell back to sleep.

Early the following morning came news from the family that her mother had died during the night, at the very time she had

had the experience – she always feels that her mother had visited her to say farewell in this beautiful manner.

Another lady wrote to me explaining that, as usual, she had woken to the alarm just before 7.00am. It was a dark December morning and her husband got up to make tea and wake the other members of the family:

'I remained in bed in the darkened room and noticed a small, white light about the size of a pinhead oscillating towards and away from my face. The intensity of the light and the regularity of the movement remained the same for a while. Then the movement faltered and became stationary and the light faded and was gone. I have experienced a variety of strange phenomena and therefore was not alarmed by this, only curious. There seemed to be no explanation.

'By 8.20am, the family had left and I was alone in the house. The telephone rang and a voice shouted, "Your mother is dead!" Since my mother had died many years earlier, I rejected this statement, but on questioning the caller a distressing story was revealed. She was the warden of a retirement home where my mother-in-law had lived, some 30 miles away. On doing her rounds at 8.00am, she had discovered that my mother-in-law had died as a result of a haemorrhage. She immediately called the doctor, who estimated her time of death to be about 7.00am.

'Many hours later, after a distressing day, I returned home and to bed. It was only then that I recalled the small, white light. By the bedroom wall hovered a vibrant, emerald-coloured sphere about the size of a small orange. It was joined by an equally brilliant blue one, and the emerald one merged with the blue one. Inside were two small dots of white light like the one I had seen that morning. It then disappeared.'[14]

Strange Feelings

On the evening of 22 May 1993, Fran Bowers and her husband Mick had a rare night out together, leaving her mum behind to babysit their 18-month-old son:

'We arrived home at about 10.00pm and Mum left at about 10.15pm – we'd had a really good night out, but from the moment we'd said goodbye to Mum and shut the door, something was wrong. Something had changed.

'I felt totally overwhelmed, restless, anxious ... but, most significantly, I felt that I'd been completely enveloped by a very heavy dark cloud of doom and I knew something bad had happened, that someone had died.

'It wasn't [just] a feeling, it was utterly and completely a feeling of certainty. I sat for the entire night on the side of my bed with the windows open and the curtains just searching the sky for answers, for hope, restless and suffocated by overwhelming doom. My husband was upset as he'd never seen me react so badly and couldn't understand when I told him.

'The following morning when Mick woke, I had had time to "plan" and told him quite directly that, if the phone went before 10.00am, he'd have to look after [our son] because I knew someone had died and worked out with weird logic that it was perhaps my granddad. As an older family member and it being my mum's dad, I would be needed to comfort and organise my mum as she would be devastated. No sooner had I finished speaking, then, as I had predicted, the phone went and it was my dad, asking us to go home as they'd had some bad news. This spooked Mick but seemed to make sense. We drove the short distance and, as I asked, Mick held our son. Dad opened the door as I stepped inside.

'I saw Mum, my sister and her twin brother sat quietly round the table. Dad stood to my left, with Mick behind me ... Dad very quietly sobbed that Martin (my half-brother aged 33 and eight years my senior) had been killed on his motorbike last night. Mick nearly passed out and said, "She knew ..." but it was so surreal that I just screamed, "NO" at the top of my voice – totally shocked because it wasn't what I'd planned ... I was so angry ... shocked, but red-mist angry – I was even angry at my granddad (I'm ashamed to say) ...

'The funeral was very public and the whole thing was covered by the media. Over 400 bikers attended his funeral, the "eternal Peter Pan".'

Injury Dreams

Chris Cherry's experience is rather different from those in the previous sections in that he dreamt not of his mother at the time of her death, but rather of the manner in which she died:

'In late November 1997, I dreamed very vividly that I had fallen and damaged my face quite seriously. I felt, in the dream, no pain whatsoever; but knew there were awful contusions and lacerations, and was terribly worried. At 6.30am my sister rang to say that my mother of 91 had died in the night from a fall down a flight of stairs in the nursing home where she was in a week's respite care. She had dementia and had been allowed to wander that night. As far as I can say, the time of my dream, and certainly the nature of the facial injuries she sustained, perfectly matched her time of death and the injuries I dreamed happening to me.'

A couple of days after the funeral of her father, Dorothy Simpson wrote how she was:

'... woken from my sleep with my [late] sister shouting my name and saying to me, "Come to the bottom of the bed." I was fully awake. I was leaning up on my arms looking for my sister, I could only see something black at the bed post, and then all this paper or feathers were floating down. I said to my sister, "I cannot move for the pain on my leg" – the pain was incredible and my leg would not move. I was still leaning up in my bed and I seemed to be wanting to take a big white sweet out of my mouth but my hand could never reach it.

The next thing I remember was telling my sister that I was dying.

'I do not know if I experienced my father's death. My lungs seemed to be filling up with a grey matter coming right up into my mouth. I knew this has to be death. I turned my head away and it was all gone.'

Death-bed visions, unprompted experiences out of the blue, remote ADCs, the manifestation of wind or light, and feeling that things just aren't quite right or dreaming about the manner of death are all common experiences and go a long way to present evidence that something does live on after our earthly body has died. In many of these instances the recipient did not know that the person had died, therefore, with this in mind, the one certainty is that it is unsafe to argue that these are all grief-induced visions or experiences.

2

TWILIGHT AND
SLEEP-STATE ADCS

*'Six weeks after his death, my father appeared to me
in a dream ... It was an unforgettable experience, and it forced
me for the first time to think about life after death'*

CARL JUNG

WE SPEND ON AVERAGE about 8 hours a day, 56 hours a
week, 224 hours a month, 122 days every year ... asleep.
That is around one-third of our lives that we are apparently doing
nothing. But is sleep really doing nothing? On the outside, it
looks like it ... a person's eyes are closed; muscles are relaxed;
breathing is regular; there is no response to sound or light.
However, if you take a look at what is happening inside the brain,
you will find quite a different situation – the brain is very active.
We enter REM (rapid-eye movement) sleep about five times in an
average eight-hour period of sleep, which means, in one year, we
will have had 1,825 dreams! Of course, we don't remember all of
these dreams, especially when you consider that an average 75-
year-old person would have about 136,875 of them, and would
have spent a total of about 25 years asleep!

Almost all cultures have looked to dreams to provide answers
to their daily lives. However, there is no single, universal dream
theory. From a spiritual point of view, dreams are a way to

connect with a higher power and offer a glimpse into the future. On the other hand, psychologists believe dreams are an extension of our waking lives. Sigmund Freud, the father of dream analysis, believed that dreams represented repressed desires and emotional conflicts in the dreamer's subconscious, which surfaced during sleep as recognisable symbols. Scientists, however, believe dreams are an attempt by the brain to make sense of the signals it receives during REM sleep. The cortex, the outer region of the brain responsible for learning, thinking and organising information, interprets these signals and creates a 'storyline' or dream.

Now, many people claim they had been contacted by a deceased loved one while they were sound asleep. This is problematic – was it a 'dream' which can be analysed by one of the above schools of thought, or is it different because it is not a 'dream' as such? Language becomes a problem because, there being no other name for their experience, respondents usually called it a 'dream'. But they will often qualify this with: 'I knew it had only been a dream but, at the same time, I knew that it had been more than a dream ...' or 'It just wasn't like an ordinary dream.'

For want of a better word, I don't want to refer to these accounts as dreams, but rather sleep-state ADCs, and they are one of the most common types of after-death communication.

As with all the accounts in this research, the experiences are spontaneous and the person dreaming has not actively sought communication. The deceased loved one attempts to communicate through dreams to give a last goodbye or a message of comfort. The recipients did not will the communication; it is as if the deceased loved one chose to communicate within the 'dream'.

The following accounts all contain sleep-state ADCs in which a deceased loved one 'broke into' what would otherwise have been an ordinary dream.

Insight
Sometimes, experiences convey information to the experiencer they did not previously know or could not otherwise have known.

Examples include the deceased locating missing money or heirlooms, or a warning to the experiencer of previously unknown danger or imminent danger. Sometimes, events are predicted or the deceased offers reassurance about a current issue which is troubling the experiencer. Some even assist in lottery wins!

Teri Bonfield took a share in a £15 million lottery prize after a dream inspired her with lottery numbers. 'A friend of mine had died of cancer ... she was 24 ...' The friend, Tina Siegel, appeared to Teri in a dream, and left her with such a strong impression of a set of numbers that she wrote them down when she awoke – 10-15-16-17-18-42 – and started playing the numbers every week.[15]

Similarly, Michael Gabriele Sr's deceased 23-year-old daughter, Cheryl, came to him in a sleep-state ADC about a month after her death in New Jersey. She said to him, 'Why don't you play the numbers? I'd like to bring you a little happiness.' When he awoke, he remembered that a New Jersey lottery slip had been found in her car. He obtained those six numbers and bought a Lotto ticket the following Saturday. That night, he won the $10.5 million first prize.[16]

A classic example of a loved one returning with a message is a case from Melvin Morse. One of his patients had a vivid dream that her son would be horribly injured in a car accident. No details were given which could have led to her preventing the accident. Indeed, she was ultimately the driver in the wreck, and the accident was her fault. She told him that the meaning of her dream to her was that her mother, who had given her the news in her dream, was her guardian angel and watched over her. She said:

> 'Without that dream, I could never have kept my family together, been a wife and a mother to my other children, because I felt so guilty and depressed over what I did. Yet I always knew that even though it was my fault, somehow it was meant to be, and my mother would always be there for me.'[17]

Such accounts have been circulating for thousands of years. In his essay *On Divination*, Marcus Tullius Cicero (106BC–43BC) reported:

> 'There were two comrades from Arcadia travelling together, and when they reached Megara one of them went to the inn, while the other accepted the hospitality of a friend.
>
> 'He and his friend finished their evening meal and retired. In his slumber, our guest dreamed that his travelling companion appeared to him and said, "The innkeeper has murdered me, flung my body into a cart and covered it with dung. Please, I beg you, be at the gate early in the morning before the cart can leave the town."
>
> Stirred to the depths of his being by this dream, he confronted at dawn the rustic who was driving the cart out of the gate. The wretch took to his heels in dismay and fright. Our friend then recovered the body and reported the murder to the proper officials. The innkeeper was duly punished.'

This is a perfect example of a sleep-state ADC because his dead friend visited him, the experiencer learned four things from the dream he could not have otherwise known – that this friend had been murdered, where and when his body could be found and who had committed the crime. This element of ESP or almost psychic unearthings does not occur to the majority of us in day-to-day dreaming.

Diane Farmer's father died in 1988 and provided her with a rather similar experience:

> 'He was cremated and there was a dispute over what to do with his ashes. I relented and agreed to my stepmother's wish that they be scattered in the garden of remembrance.
>
> 'Two years later, I had a dream. I was speaking with

the funeral director and he told me I hadn't buried my father properly ... [and other personal predictions all of which have come true]. In 1996, after a series of events and dreams restating the above, I went to visit my stepmother to ask her what she had done with my father's ashes. She replied, "They are in the funeral parlour." I immediately went and got my father's ashes.

'I was told that one month later and they would have been dumped on the council tip. I cast his ashes in the Thames.'

Another event occurred in 2001 when Diane was preparing to return to live with her lover in France. The night before she was to arrange removal, she dreamt of her father. 'It was a terrifying dream, but I understood the message due to the very precise symbolism ... it led me to uncover that my love was deceiving me.'

John Wyborn wrote:

'Way back in the 1940s when I was a young boy, I would spend many holidays with a young cousin who lived with his parents and with my grandmother, a very loving person who was devoted to both her grandchildren, and especially close to the daughter and grandchild with whom she lived. Eventually, in the winter of 1944, she died of a sudden illness. We were all very sad, and especially my aunt, who was truly devastated for some time afterwards. She told us that she would occasionally have dreams about her deceased mother.

'In one of these dreams, our grandmother was with her at a party, at which she saw many other relatives whom she knew and who had also died. In addition, there were a number of strangers. Just as she was about to awake, it suddenly came to my aunt that "these were all the others, the great grandparents we never knew". In another dream, my grandmother turned to her and said in the dream, "This is how I intend to keep in touch with you girls if I can."

'In due course, my aunt, like the rest of us, recovered from the bereavement, and life had to go on. As far as I know, no one had any more dreams involving my grandmother for the next 50 years. I have always cherished her memory, and occasionally asked myself in moments of stress, "What would Granny have said or done?" but nothing more than that.

'Then one night, about four or five years ago, she appeared quite suddenly in a dream of mine. I had been absorbed in some gathering of people in my dream, the details of which I cannot recall, when I gradually became aware of my grandmother sitting quietly to one side in a chair. After a while, I tore myself away from whatever I had been doing and told myself I really must go over to her. She had been there all the time and I had been ignoring her. I ran over to her, and put my arms around her, saying, "We shall all be together again one day, shan't we?" To my dismay, she looked straight ahead into the distance and said sadly, "Oh no. Oh no." Then I awoke.

'It was a haunting dream and a puzzling one, but I put it behind me like one does, and thought little of it. Then some six months later, I found myself in conversation with a member of the Church's Fellowship for Psychical Studies who is well known for his psychic and sensitive powers, and somewhat casually I asked him about this dream. After carrying out some simple processes, he assured me that my grandmother was all right, but that she certainly was very perturbed about something. He could not say what it was, but it probably had something to do with our family. I was not to worry, but to pray for her and await developments calmly. Was anyone in our family unwell?

'Some nine months after that conversation, I had a telephone call out of the blue from my cousin, the only other one of our immediate family still alive that my grandmother knew and with whom she had lived. Although still in touch, we had rather drifted apart over the years, as cousins do, and did not meet all that often. He had good news that a grandchild of his was on the way. He also had bad news, in that he had cancer, diagnosed four or five months previously.

'To cut a long story short, he died last year. I had written at the time of his telephone call and told him of my dream experience, but mentioning – since he was a practising Christian, as am I – that I was aware that not everyone found this type of thing helpful. I said that I would not refer to it again unless he did. He never did refer to it in the next few times we communicated or met after that ... nonetheless, I am convinced that my grandmother had some kind of perception of the future events that were about to unfold. I believe she felt impelled to share them with the only other person still alive from those days in the 1940s, using a means of communication that she had found open to her before. I can only hope and pray that I was of some comfort to her.'

Dreams of Comfort

Other sleep-state ADCs provide the simple message that all is well – Linda Appleby's brother-in-law died in 1980 at the age of 26. She simply '... had a dream that he was sitting down calmly in front of me and that the message was that he was happy'.

Heather Bliss had an ADC with her father:

'He died in July 1996 after his second heart bypass without regaining consciousness. Rather unfortunately for me, I knew about a month earlier that this was his

time and he would not survive. I think he knew, too.
Anyway, that September I had a strange experience
with a dream that wasn't a dream. I was with Dad and
we were stood there just hugging each other. I could
feel him and smell him (and he was very hairy) and
there was no background except white. I was not
looking down on this scene as I usually do in dreams –
usually watching myself rather than being myself, but I
was as I am now – within my own body and feeling
sensations I normally would. I know it was not a dream
and I know that it was my father coming to say
goodbye. He knew that I believe in life after death and
that I would be open to his visit.

'I have obviously had other dreams about him, but
none the same as that one. Interestingly, a friend of mine
had a similar dream in which she saw her dead father and
went running into his arms – only her background was
grey and not white, but she felt it the same as I did – that
was not a dream ...'

Another letter came from a nurse who became a bereaved mother
when she lost her four-year-old son, Toby, from a brain
haemorrhage:

'This occurred approximately one year after my son
died. I recall the dream as if I had just had it last night. I
was standing on a river bank and looking over at Toby
on the other side.

'His side was a lush green with beautiful trees. The
water was a beautiful blue, and there were birds I could
hear. It was a paradise, like the Garden of Eden.
Everything was so quiet and peaceful. Toby was standing
in grass and flowers up to his waist, close to the edge of
the river. He was a little boy, the same little guy that I
lost. He was wearing a striped T-shirt and blue jeans and

was so very real and happy. I kept trying to get over to Toby, but I couldn't. He looked up at me and spoke with such calmness. He said, "No, Mum, you can't come over here. I'm OK. I'm fine. But you can't come over here." He had to tell me that several times because I wanted to cross the river to be with him. Toby was calming me like an adult would. I almost felt like a child in comparison, as if an older, wiser person was talking to me. He was telling me to settle down and realise that his life is good now. He gave me the sense that he is at peace and that he's where he belongs. The dreams seemed so real, as real as life itself.

'When I woke up, I felt crushed that the dream was over. And yet I felt so comforted by it.'

Norma Parfitt's grandmother had been deaf throughout her life, and when she visited her in a dream, she was delighted that she could now hear her. Her brother visited her in several dreams, leaving an 'undescribable peace'. Her mother-in-law also visited in a dream, 'seeing her at a much younger age, so she had to tell me who she was. My uncle by marriage actually showed himself to me twice and often helped me out.'

Jenny Brook's husband died some time ago, and about seven months later she had, as she explains it, a vivid waking dream:

'It was as if there was a blank, white wall, when suddenly a door opened outwards towards me and there was my husband as he was in his early twenties (he was 47 when he died of cancer). He smiled at me and [his] eyes were looking straight at me. A voice called from over my shoulder: "It's Nick!" I immediately awoke and lay in the dark with the most wonderful loving feeling around me and ... golden lights dancing all around me, like rays. I interpreted this as him being recovered from a rest time following all his pain and letting me know he was around again. I often feel his presence and experience the golden lights.'

After the death of Carol Stewart's young son, and a couple of years after her brother died, she '... saw them both in a dream and my brother was reaching out to hold the hands of my son. As if they'd both found one another in the afterlife.'

A couple of years before her dad died, Veronica Mooney had a dream about her nan who had died a while ago:

> 'She said, "Ask your dad if he will forgive Eileen," ... that was my dad's sister, she had died. My dad and Eileen were not on very good speaking terms for years. I told my dad and he said he had forgiven her.
>
> 'Then in 2001, Dad died of lung cancer. Just before his death, Nan came again in a dream and said, "I am coming to take your father away." I said, "We need him here with us ..." His dad, mum, sister and brothers had all passed away, he was the last one left. I said, "Nan, please let him stay with us for ten years more. There is so much we have not done with Dad yet. We all want to go to Florida as a family for the last time." She replied, "All his family need him here now."
>
> 'A few weeks after the funeral, Dad visited me in a dream. He said, "I really liked what you did for the funeral." We had a woman funeral director walking in front of the coffin. He said, "That was a novel idea, it did make me laugh." '

Agnes O'Reilly talked about when her mother suffered a stroke and died on 2 September 1982:

> 'I travelled from England to the West of Ireland to attend the funeral. We were all devastated by the loss of our mum; however, the fact that she often told me that she

had a fear of dying weighed heavily on my mind. I have always believed in life after death though this did not ease my worry about how my mother was dealing with her new experience. All day, every day, I thought about my mother.

'On the morning of 15 October 1982, at approximately 5.30am, my mother came to me as I was in that phase as you drift in and out of sleep. She talked to me about her death, she explained to me in great detail how she died and said she did not know what was happening to her until she saw her sister Mary and her mother and father, then she realised that she was dead.

'I then opened my eyes, and sat up in bed – my mother was there by the bed all dressed in white, feet not touching the floor. Her last words to me were, "But I'm happy now," with a great big smile, she looked so happy. The vision I shall never forget. When I checked it out with my sister at a later date, she said [mother's death] happened exactly as my mother had told me.

'It brought much peace and consolation to my aching heart. I have never had a dream about my mother since that morning. I know she's happy now ... that makes me happy, too.

'I had a similar message from my father John who died in 1993, 11 years after my mother. He had suffered from osteoporosis for about 20 years ... at the time of his death, he had gone from 5ft 11in tall to a stooped 4ft 10in. I often wondered how he was, then had a lovely surprise to see this youthful man, so tall, slim and wearing a cream-coloured mac as he tipped his hat, smiling broadly, to say, "I'm no longer suffering from osteoporosis." It is comforting to know that my loved ones are happy and I'm so grateful that they let me know.'

Steve Cowling writes:

'When I was 18, it was discovered I had a congenitally deformed gall bladder and it was decided to operate to remove it. My father had died about six months previously and I was a dental student at Guy's Hospital, London. The night before the operation, I had a dream which has stayed with me ever since. It was the most vivid and real dream. I saw the colour of everything, felt movement, touch and smell. Such was the lifelike feeling of it all.

'I was on a train that was being pulled by a steam engine. I felt the movement as it made its way through a beautiful green valley, Sheep grazed in fields and I heard them bleat in the sunshine. I was not alone on the train. The carriage was packed with other people. Nobody spoke but there was an air of expectancy and everyone appeared to be happy. Eventually, the train drew to a halt and the carriage I was in gradually emptied as the passengers alighted on to a small platform. I followed them and, as everyone seemed to be waiting, I stood with them. The station was small and the engine steamed and hissed as it stood by the platform. At the back of the platform was a small fence and beyond that the countryside gradually sloped upwards to a ridge a short distance away. Suddenly, the crowd became quite excited and I saw one or two pointing in the direction of the ridge. I turned and saw many people running towards the station, waving and laughing. There was a small wicket gate in the fence and when the first of these visitors arrived, he opened it and the people on the platform ran through. There was a great deal of hugging and excited chatter as everyone greeted each other.

'Eventually, the group moved away and disappeared over the ridge leaving me alone on the station platform. The engine continued its hissing.

Then I looked towards the ridge again to see a lone figure approaching. As he got closer, I realised it was my father and I ran to the fence. He ran towards me and we held each other tight. I can still feel his arms around me. I asked him if he was all right and he said everything was wonderful and that he was being treated well. Then he said I was to ask the surgeon to remove my appendix as well as the gall bladder. He told me "it was all in the appendix". He turned to go and I moved to follow him through the gate. He turned, placed his hand on my chest and told me to stay where I was, that it was not my time. I watched him leave, returned to the train carriage and woke up.

The following day, I asked the surgeon if he would remove my appendix while he operated on the gall bladder. He agreed to do so and later told me it was a good job my appendix had been removed. It was about 6in in length and ready to cause trouble.

'All that happened when I was 18. I am now 54 and, while I can remember other dreams, this one remains as vivid as when I dreamt it. As a postscript, I became seriously ill about two years ago and was close to death.'

A Final Goodbye

Often when a loved one passes we have not had the opportunity to tell them specifically how much they mean to us, or indeed appreciate how much we meant to them, the following accounts are all ADCs whereby the deceased returned to reiterate and provide closure, to say a final goodbye.

Lora[18] described how at the end of her dream she felt loved and finally knew that her grandma did love her which she wasn't sure about prior to the experience.

'Grandma and I were never close. She got me spanked for something she said I did but I didn't and as a kid I had a hard time forgetting it. When Grandma died I felt bad. But that's OK, she wasn't suffering any more.

One night I went to sleep and Grandma came to me in a dream ... She took me shopping and was driving a car (Grandma never drove a car). She took me out to lunch and we had a wonderful time and really had a wonderful afternoon. Suddenly we were in front of my home and Grandma stopped the car and looked at me and said, "Honey, I had to work all my life and we never got a chance to do these things and I would have loved to but couldn't. I came to tell you I love you." She kissed me and said, "Bye, sweetie." I remember whispering as I was waking up, "Bye, Grandma, I love you too."

On 31 January 1998, Mary Malcolmson's 22-year-old son died. He'd arrived home one evening claiming he'd had a fall from 20ft and was hurting in his stomach. Mary and her husband Ian took him to the Casualty department and, because he said that he'd fallen from such a height, he was transported by ambulance to a major hospital a few miles away:

'The hospital didn't think that he had fallen but they decided to keep him in overnight for observations. We were told he had admitted to experimenting with drugs and we left him in their care overnight. As I kissed my beautiful son goodbye, I little realised that it would be the last time I would see him alive.

'I fully hoped that I would have been able to go and collect him after I had finished work the next day. Around 4.00pm, I received a call from the hospital saying that my son's condition throughout the day had deteriorated and, whilst they were trying to do an emergency scan on him, he had collapsed with massive internal injuries. He never regained consciousness and, four days later in the intensive care unit, he died. As you can imagine, my world stopped.

'Three mornings later, I woke up and then slipped back into a light sleep. The next thing I knew was that I was still in bed but my son was with me. I felt his weight on top of me and his head was buried in my neck. I didn't see his face but, as my arms came around him, I knew from the feel of him, without a shadow of a doubt, that it was him and I knew that he had come to say goodbye. I even pictured the clothes he was wearing. He always liked good-quality clothes and the thickness of the t-shirt that he appeared to have on was one that I was very familiar with. I knew in my dream that he had died and I knew that I realised my hold on him would go to the spirit world.

'[When] I woke up, I knew it had only been a dream but at the same time I knew that it had been more than a dream and that I'd been given the chance to say goodbye.

'I had one more dream and that took place three or four days after the new millennium. I was walking in the corridor at work when, all of a sudden, he was there in front of me. Again, I knew he was dead and in my dream I went towards him with my arms outstretched. He had a beautiful smile on his face and he seemed to shine. The thing that struck me in the dream was how clear his face was ... it had been so long since I had seen his face (I can't look at photos of him as it upsets me too much ... we'd had a very special relationship). He just looked at me, grinned and said, "Happy New Year, Mum."'

Jackie Robinson wrote:

'Gramps and I were very close and it hit me very hard when he died; I was 21 at the time. What troubled me for days after his death was that I had never got around to telling Gramps that I loved him.

'One evening, I had a dream that was so real it still feels like yesterday, even though it was 18 years ago. I dreamt that my younger sister Julie went to the Chapel of Rest and stole his body from the coffin. We hoisted him up on to our shoulders, crossed over the road at the pedestrian crossing and waited for a number 32 bus to come to take us home. We boarded the bus once it arrived and took Gramps upstairs. When we arrived at our destination, we brought him back downstairs and proceeded to carry him home to my house which was about 15 minutes' walk away.

'Once we got him home, we took him up to my bedroom and laid him on the bed. From this point, Julie disappeared and Gramps and I were alone. He was lying with his legs folded down over the bed so I could kneel down beside him and see him properly. I took hold of his hands and said, "Gramps, I love you." He immediately opened his eyes, looked straight at me and very simply said, "I know you do."

'From then on, I no longer worried that I'd never taken the time to tell him; this for me was Gramps's way of letting me know he'd always known I loved him and to stop worrying.'

Alison Myers has had several similarly vivid dreams:

'I have had three dreams in which I have met and talked with deceased members of my family. The first two have been very comforting.

The first dream was early in 1986 when I was 22. My mum had died in June 1985 and, in February 1986, I bought my first house with help from my dad. Shortly after I moved in, I dreamt that Mum came to visit. In the dream, we walked through the rooms in my house and she told me how much she liked it. We discussed things like the curtains, my crockery and how I had the furniture arranged. As is sometimes the case in dreams, the details of the house in the dream didn't match my house in real life, but in the dream it was definitely my house that I was showing her around! What Mum conveyed to me in the time we seemed to be together was how pleased she was for me that I'd bought my first home and that she fully approved of it. She wanted me to know that, even though she wasn't physically there when I moved in, she was with me in spirit.

'When I woke the next morning, I felt tremendously uplifted from having spent time with her and from knowing that she still knew what was happening in my life and was happy for me.

'The second dream was early in 2000, only a few weeks after my brother had suddenly tragically died. Our relationship had been somewhat strained during the preceding few years on account of his fundamental Christian beliefs, and I was devastated by his death and the impossibility of ever being reconciled to him in this life. In the dream, I found myself sitting with him in a bedroom of the last family home he and I had lived in together (before either of us had left home). We were sitting on two beds that were side by side, facing each other and having a heart-to-heart. We talked about issues in his relationship with his girlfriend (who later became his wife and widow) and I took him to task about some things.

'The strange thing is that we had had a similar heart-to-heart in real life which had occurred after he was married, but once again, in the strange way of dreams, it seemed quite natural to be in the past setting of our family home but talking about things that had only happened later and that we couldn't have known about when we lived in that house. The overall effect of the dream was that I woke with a strong sense that I'd spent some time with him and that, despite our recent differences which had led to a breakdown in communication, underneath we remained close and loved one another. It was a very comforting dream and I felt as if it had gone some way towards a resolution of our differences.'

So, as can be seen, these 'dreams' are not the usual kind of nightly dreams we usually encounter. As the Guggenheims point out, 'There are many significant differences between an ordinary dream and a sleep-state ADC. A dream is generally fragmented, jumbled, filled with symbolism and incomplete in various ways. Though some are very intense emotionally, they typically have a quality of unreality about them and are often soon forgotten.'[18]

In contrast, sleep-state ADCs feel like actual face-to-face visits with deceased loved ones. They are much more orderly, colourful, vivid and memorable than most dreams. In fact, some may be after-death visions that just occur during sleep ...

3

MESSAGES FROM THE OTHER SIDE

'Death ends a life, not a relationship'

JACK LEMMON

LEADING ON FROM THE sleep-state chapter, this section deals with specific messages whereby the loved one has returned to impart information or to let someone know that all is well. In some instances, occurrences convey information to the experiencer which they did not or could not have previously known. Some are way out like the case whereby one woman was visited by a dead male friend who asked her to tell his wife to look for an insurance policy she didn't know about hidden in a chest in the bedroom. When his wife looked, the policy was there. Other examples of such communication include the location of missing objects or reassurance. Sometimes events are predicted or the deceased simply returns to say that all is well.

Some accounts are more dramatic and actually alert the recipient to a previously unknown danger or imminent danger. One morning, for example, Grayce Shapiro placed a tea kettle on her gas stove and fell asleep. Her deceased husband, Billie, alerted her in a sleep-state ADC that she was in danger. She awoke immediately and found that the stove's pilot light was off and her kitchen was filled with gas.

Similarly, a story close to Lois Bunker Woods heart has been relayed to her from her mother. When Lois was an 18-month-old toddler she was about to drink an arsenic solution that was used on the dairy farm that was her home. Her recently deceased grandmother alerted her mother to this imminent danger through an auditory ADC. Her mother followed the voice and dashed outside – just in time to protect Lois from drinking this deadly poison.

Lost ... and Found

Mrs Almond finds her contact with the spirit realm helps her to make the right decisions. 'It's great if I lose an item ... they help me to find it.'

Verena Winearl's granny has also assisted when important items have gone astray, and when turning the house upside down had not uncovered the lost item. 'My paternal grandmother, who brought me up, died seven years ago, but I often get the feeling she is watching me. She doesn't exactly have conversations with me, but I feel she does guide me in certain situations when I need a bit of help!'

On one occasion, Verena and her husband were due to fly to Antigua to attend a friend's wedding. But, with only two weeks to go and the whole thing paid for, she suddenly realised she could not find her husband's passport and wasn't even sure it was still valid:

> 'Not wanting to admit this to him, fearing the usual "Why didn't you do it earlier?" etc., I started searching for it. We have a filing cabinet where it would normally have been kept, but it was not there. I looked in every cupboard and drawer in the entire house and then through all the suitcases, travel bags, coats and handbags ... to no avail. The next day, I went through the same

routine again because, although I had already searched everywhere I could think of, I just had to find it!

'I was upstairs in our bedroom, again looking through the travel bags, when for no apparent reason I raced down the stairs into the kitchen. I saw my gran standing beside the pine dresser ... it stands in a corner, but because of the radiator there is a very small gap between it and one wall. I reached down there and pulled out a very tatty carrier bag full of old receipts and other bits of paper. Also in there was the passport! Then I remembered, six months previously, I had had to take my husband's passport into our bank for them to photocopy it, so I'd had it in my handbag.

'That night, I had had a phone call to say that my father had died in Germany and I had to go over there the next day. I took out everything I did not need to take with me from my handbag, stuffed it into a carrier bag and put it beside the dresser. I heard my gran telling me off for not having put it away properly – she was always berating me for not putting things away the very minute I had finished using them.'

Another occasion was when she needed to make a couple of photocopies for the business and, at the same time, needed to send a copy of the car registration document to the insurance company.

'I drove to the village post office and did all the copies at the same time. I keep all the car documents in a folder marked "Mercedes" and duly returned the original registration document back into the folder. About a month later, I desperately needed the photocopied page I had made for the business, but could not find it anywhere, even after the usual scramble through all my hidey-holes! I then heard my gran saying, "Mercedes."

Mercedes? I thought. I raced out to the drive and looked in the car – in the glove box, under all the seats, everywhere, but it was not there. "Haven't got it right this time, have you?" I told her. With that, I seemed to be frog-marched into our office straight to the filing cabinet. Yes, it was in the "Mercedes" file, stuffed in behind the registration document I had copied at the same time! Granny had come up trumps once again!'

Finally, Verena's gran had left her a very pretty, 18-carat gold bracelet, which she wore daily as a reminder of her, rather than just keeping it in a jewellery box. It had a snap-shut clasp and two security hinges:

'One day, I was in the kitchen unloading the dishwasher, when I suddenly found myself walking up to the very end of our quite large garden. I walked straight over to a part that is not really used much, bent down and in the grass saw what looked like my bracelet. I immediately looked at my wrist to make sure it was mine, as I had not even realised I'd lost it. As I picked it up, I could hear my gran telling me I should have taken better care of it. What struck me as very strange was that the bracelet, covered in mud, was completely fastened with the clasp and both security hinges.'

In a similar situation to Verena, Chris Cherry wasn't aware that something was actually missing until he had a dream after his father-in-law died in 1975 after surgery.

'The night after his death – or possibly the night after that – I had a vivid dream in which he appeared in bright sun at my sitting-room window while I was reading. He was standing in what I can only describe as the kind of hydraulic lift used by telephone engineers and electricians to service street lamps. He was smiling and relaxed, but repeatedly pointed to his left wrist. I took him to be asking the time, and gave it to him. He then "swung away" in his contraption.

'I mentioned the dream to my wife upon waking. The next day, my mother-in-law rang us to say, in some consternation, that [her husband's] watch was not among his hospital bits and pieces ... it turned up a day or two later.'

Reassurance over Current Events

Zimbabwe's President, Robert Mugabe, has been seeing someone new for the last six months. Josiah Tongogara was once a serious political rival of the President and, most shockingly of all, Tongogara has been dead since 1980. It seems that Mugabe has been 'seeing' him in the most literal sense of late, consistently catching sight of his ghost, much to his alarm. He now insists that a place is set for Tongogara at every meal, and bemused staff are forced to serve food to the empty chair. Mugabe is said to believe that the former guerrilla leader is tormenting him with accusations that his mismanagement has destroyed the revolution they fought for together. This does seem a little harsh, if one disregards the fact that the regime crippled the economy, reduced the nation to a state of lawless anarchy, oppressed most of the population, resulted in countless atrocities and murders and has seen the power-crazed President ride roughshod over democratic principles. Mugabe is now said to employ several witch doctors, a rain goddess and an oracle to help him run the country.[19]

On his first day in the White House as the 26th President of the United States, Theodore Roosevelt felt his father's presence and his hand on his shoulder as he signed his first official papers. That evening, as his sisters and their husbands attended dinner, each of the men was presented with a yellow saffonia rose. President Roosevelt exclaimed with surprise, "Isn't that strange! This is the rose we all connect with our father." [20]

Moira McKenzie remembers a time when 'I was going through a bad phase regarding a family matter when [my grandfather] contacted me. He told me all would work out fine. I saw him in great detail, it was as if he was alive and not in spirit. I could see every detail of the clothes he was wearing. What he said did come true.'

Donald Campbell, the former British car and speedboat racer, believed in life after death. He spoke on a number of occasions of feeling the presence of his dead father, Sir Malcolm Campbell, with him in the cockpit of his boats and rocket cars. As he sat in the cockpit of *Bluebird* and prepared to achieve his 403mph (648kph) land-speed record on Lake Eyre salt flats in Australia, he saw his father's spirit: 'He was crystal-clear and looked down at me with the half-smile on his face I knew so well.'

Then he heard the spirit say, 'Well, boy, now you know how I felt on the morning of 2 September at Utah in 1935.' That was the day his father burst a tyre at over 300mph (480kph). His father's voice encouraged Donald Campbell. Like his father before him, Donald became the holder of both the water and land-speed records. [21]

When General George S Patton was pinned down by machine-gun fire during the Battle of the Argonne in World War I, he saw his deceased grandfather and great-uncles in the sky looking down on him with disapproval. This inspired him to draw his revolver and rally 300 infantrymen in a tank attack against the Germans, for which he later received the Distinguished Service Cross.

General Patton also briefly described several occasions when his father, who died of tuberculosis in 1927, visited him in his tent in the evenings, in France during World War II. The two men sat down and talked, and his father assured him he would act bravely and perform well in the next day's battle. The General said about his father, 'He was just as real as in his study at home.'[22]

Gloomy Predictions

A woman who called Jerrod Zelanka's house early Sunday was crying and her voice was faint. 'I'm at the bottom of a dark hole,' the woman said. Then the line went dead. Jerrod dialled the code used to automatically trace the number of the caller, but the number came up as withheld.

Now, Jerrod and others think that call somehow was made by his friend, 20-year-old Leah Jean Ash, after she and a friend had an accident in an all terrain bike. She was a passenger on the three-wheel vehicle. Both were found dead early Sunday on the bank of a drainage canal after an accident.

The strange part is neither Ash nor her friend driving carried a mobile phone that night. Police divers checked the shallow canal to see whether there was a telephone, but found nothing. A subpoena was obtained to get the telephone records of the call made that night to Jerrod's house but it came up with nothing.

The accident happened towards the end of a rainy evening during which six friends took turns riding the Yamaha Banshee 350cc at a construction site. The man driving Leah was an experienced all-terrain-vehicle driver, but was apparently blinded by the rain and made a turn while traveling about 30mph. When the two didn't return, Mike Taylor, Leah's boyfriend, began to worry. He and the others called police and tried looking for them in the dark. Finally, about 6am on Sunday, Jerrod and a schoolmate of Leah, found the bodies after a two-hour search in his four-wheel-drive truck.[23]

Chris Johnson wrote:

'My son Ray (my second son, aged 20) died in August 1989. Before he died, I lost a close friend, the mother of my third son. The "spooky" events did not fall into place until after Ray's death ... he played numeral tricks or games to let me know he had survived. Ray sent me a £20,000 sales lead (that paid for his funeral and helped us survive the business losses) then told me how to spend his commission. He warned of a rip-off ... I lost £1.8m ...'

A contributor who did not wish to be named wrote:

'There are many other times when other relatives have contacted me, especially in dreams and usually if someone else is in trouble. A few years ago my Uncle Hal kept popping into my mind. He lived about 60 miles away in Birmingham. That night in my dream, my nan (Uncle Hal's sister) came to me with a very definite message for him ... scolding him and basically telling me to tell him that "They're not ready for him yet" and to "buck up".

The next morning, I went to my mum's to tell her of my dream and what Nan had said, as I usually do. I found her on the phone to Uncle Hal, who'd phoned, desperate, frightened and very depressed. We told him of my dream and he cried. Then he told us that he'd hidden my Aunty Lil's Alzheimer's Disease for four years but couldn't cope any longer, but after 50 years of marriage didn't want to be separated. We intervened and

supported them at home for a further two years until my
Uncle Hal's last and terminal illness.'

General Messages

Not all messages offer dramatic insights; some are more mundane
but are of equal importance to the recipient. One lady described
how 'my granddad who passed over two years ago came to me in
a dream with specific lists of things to be done – which were
verified later in his will. He also told me he wasn't leaving the
house until it was all sorted to my satisfaction. My sister bought
the house which felt totally right, but initially the only music she
could get to play was classical, which was my grandfather's great
passion in life.'

Sylvie Singerz and her sister were very close. She recalls, 'I
have seen her in my home and received some messages for her
daughter. I always get a certain smell (of pot pourri) before she
appears and all the messages have been meaningful and
accurate.' Barbara Valliant has also experienced messages from
the other side:

'My mum passed away three years ago and the first time
I felt her come to me was just a few days after she died.
I was crying and said out loud, "I just want to give you a
cuddle." That night, I dreamt that she gave me a cuddle
and I felt a lot calmer when I woke.

'I was suffering again badly a few months later and,
again, said out loud, "I just miss talking to you," and
dreamt again that she came and talked to me for a long
while. During our conversation, I said Dad was upset
because he could not face going to the grave. She told
me to tell him she should not have said what she said to
him and her mother had told her off when she had got
there. I told Dad this and, when he could speak though
his tears, he told me she had said, "Don't leave my grave
cold like you left your mother's." She also said that my

sister's little boy was beautiful ... my little sister was six months' pregnant when Mum died.'

Paul McCartney, who lost his wife Linda to breast cancer in 1998, says he's comforted by thoughts that her spirit lives on. 'After Linda died, I think all of us in the family would hear noises or see things and think, "That's Linda, that's Mum ... and I think, in some ways, it's very comforting to think she's still here.'

Paul said he has been compelled to write poetry since her death, including a poem called *Her Spirit*, in which Linda's spirit visits him in the woods, in the form of a white squirrel. 'You don't know if it's true, but it's a great thought. And it's an uplifting thought. So I allow myself to go there,' Paul says. He has since published an anthology of poetry entitled *Blackbird Singing*, inspired by experiences ranging from his early Liverpool memories to the loss of Linda.[24]

Chris Bartlett's story was similar to Paul McCartney's in that he, too, gained inspiration. His mother died, aged 70, after a heart-attack:

'Of course, I was very upset but my father, brothers and sister were far worse than me. They continued to grieve for ages and could not talk about our mother's death at all. I just wasn't affected so strongly, but that's not to say that I didn't miss her – I still do, naturally – but I didn't feel so strongly until about a week or so later ... it was a Saturday afternoon.

'Before I carry on, I must tell you that I have always loved the piano and I have been having lessons for many years now. I know I will never be that good but I do enjoy what I do. I have even been able to compose quite a few simple but I think quite nice little tunes.

'It was a Saturday afternoon when I was practising at the piano, when suddenly a tune and even some words came into my head. I started to play the tune and tried to sing the words and it seemed that all the grief just flooded out of me all at once. The tears just fell, even on to the keyboard. When I got over the initial feeling, I could not really believe that this was all maybe from my mother, but I like to think it was. I will always remember that day.

'I wrote down the music and the words, albeit it rather crudely, I took them to my piano teacher and asked him if we could polish them up, we did this and I was quite pleased with the words and the music, which were in hymn form, with four verses and a chorus. After a few more adjustments, it was played and sung as part of the service that was held for my mother in her church. I will always feel that my mother sent it to me.'

Sitting Tenants

The Gibbs, of Bee Gees fame, lived in an old Oxfordshire house where priests used to train to become bishops. Robin-John, the Gibbs' son, is said by his mother, Dwina Murphy-Gibb, to see the phantoms of their house's ex-inhabitants.

According to Dwina, the four-year-old boy described John and Mary who lived there and their friend Elizabeth. 'He had no framework for historical costume, but he told me Mary wore a dress down to her ankles. He also said one of the children had never grown up. I discovered a very detailed account of a John and Mary Rose who once lived on the site. They had two children, one of whom died in infancy.' [25]

In 1974, Maurice Watkinson moved to a village called Holcombe Brook. He explains:

'As was usual, my mother-in-law came to stay with us (especially during the winters) for long periods, and so knew our house very well. Unfortunately, in September 1977, she died as a result of an unfortunate accident – she had removed the base of a dining chair in order to repair the tapestry seat. She was busy watching television at the same time, walked backwards to the chair and sat down, falling through the frame of the chair base and becoming trapped. Although she endeavoured to attract attention, no one heard her and she was not found until the following morning. She was then taken to the local hospital but was returned to her flat the same morning as no injuries could be found. Her eldest son and his wife came over from York to stay with her, but unfortunately she died two days later through exhaustion.

'In October of the same year, we found the bungalow we wanted and moved there in November. In addition to buying our house, our buyers also bought our bedroom furniture – it being too big for our bungalow.

'A year or so later, my wife was in the vicinity of our old house, talking to an ex-neighbour of ours who then told my wife that the lady in our old house was not very happy living there, whereupon my wife said she could not understand why, for we had been very happy and only moved as it was a rather large place just for the two of us. The neighbour then said that it was due to the lady of the house waking up during the night and finding a little grey-haired old lady sat at the foot of the bed. My wife's response was, "Good heavens! We forgot to let her know where we were moving to!" '

Michelle Gilbert wrote:

> 'One night after we moved in [to our new house], I
> thought I would take down the old net curtains and buy
> some more ... that night, I went to bed and nearly
> dropped off to sleep [when I] realised I'd not drawn the
> curtains, then I saw something very strange – it was faces
> at my bedroom window. Some faces I knew and some I
> didn't know at all, then things started to happen like
> strange smells in the house and then someone walking
> around my bed. Then these faces started to appear on
> my bedroom walls. They were just looking at me, then
> about four weeks ago they disappeared, but I still don't
> know why they were there.'

'I'm OK!'

Pauline Audoir's mother sat in the chair of the living room and
said, 'I'm all right, Paul', three days after her passing.

Pam James took her mum into hospital on Monday, 20
December 1993 to have an X-ray as she had a blockage in her leg
and her little toe had 'died':

> 'Whilst we were waiting for the nurse to admit her, she
> looked up at
> me. She was in an armchair and I was standing directly
> in front of her holding her hands. Apart from Mum's bad
> legs and arthritis, she was a very intelligent, alert, 80-
> year-old, lovely lady.
> 'She looked up at me and said, "Ruth (my sister) and I
> have been arranging my service." I was so shocked by
> this that I said, "Mum, whatever do you mean?"
> although, of course, I actually knew but didn't want to
> hear it! "What hymns I want," she replied. "Oh don't be
> silly," I said, "it is Christmas and the angels will be too
> busy singing carols to be singing hymns," was all I could

Robbie Williams has been having spiritual encounters since he was a small boy, claims his dad, mostly in the pub in which he grew up:

> 'The one that really frightened me was when I'd locked up at lunchtime and was taking him out,' publican Pete Conway said. 'We walked along the corridor and were looking into the bar. There was nobody about and the door was locked, but you could see through the window. As Robbie looked into the bar, he said, "What are those two men still doing in the bar? I don't think I like them." I thought, Here we go again. I'm looking at the bar and there's nobody there, but he's backing away a little bit. So I said, "They can stay there until I get back," and told him to wave bye-bye to them. He waved, but he stepped back, saying, "They've got no hands, Dad." '

The former Take That star has often said he feels uneasy in hotels because he can feel spirits. 'A hotel is full of ghosts,' he once said. 'I can't sleep there if I'm on my own. I'm scared of walking down the corridor.'

What is particularly interesting is that Robbie also claims he is haunted by the ghosts of his idol Frank Sinatra, and his nan Betty, who passed away not so long ago. 'She used to say she'd come back, and I feel her with me.'[26]

say. Then suddenly my "voice" that sometimes tells me things said, "Go on, say it ... go on, say it," and I found myself saying to Mum, "But, Mum, if you do go and there is another side, please, please will you come back and give me a sign?" "Yes," she said. "Say something about anemones," I said, but when I said this last bit the nurse had just walked in and I knew I had lost her attention. (Anemones in our family have always been called as they are spelled – *an-e-mones* – and I associate them with her.)

'Mum had an operation on the Wednesday to repair a blockage in her leg. They took a vein that ran all the way down her leg and turned it round to be an artery. Unfortunately, on the Friday morning (Christmas Eve) my two sisters and I were called to the hospital in the morning as the site had erupted and she was haemorrhaging and was on her way to theatre. When we arrived, as we were walking into the hospital I just knew that her spirit was leaving her body – I said nothing to my sisters.

'We were taken into a room where a nurse said that her chances of survival were very slim but I knew she was just really "preparing us" for the news. The surgeon then came into the room and I remember feeling very indignant and thinking, Why aren't you with my mother? and then I thought, I know why ...

'He told us he was very sorry but she had not survived, whereupon I burst into uncontrollable tears as Mum had been my absolute rock and saviour. (I had gone through a very nasty divorce in 1986 and was a single mum with two sons of 18 and 19.)

'A little while later, we were given a cup of tea or coffee ... I was in complete shock. We had only really expected Mum to have been in a few days so this was just so unexpected. I remember sitting with my empty cup and saucer on my lap and looking out at the blue sky and white clouds and thinking to myself, Oh, it's a lovely day. With that, Mum spoke to me so loudly and clearly and precisely that I jumped.

' "I'm all right, I'm all right!" she said in such a loud, insistent voice and it was definitely her voice. I jumped and held my hand to my throat because I could feel my heart beating and looked towards my sisters who were talking to the nurse and surgeon. They obviously had not heard it and I was amazed but I knew they hadn't because they did not react. When I told them later, they were both a bit sceptical and asked why they hadn't heard her voice. I said I really didn't know, but wondered if it had been because I had asked her on the Monday. Although, to be honest, I never expected her to die then anyway, and hadn't really expected a sign.

'When I arrived home at about 4.00pm that day, my sons were with their father. I walked into the lounge and said out loud, "Mum, this is what I bought you for Christmas [it was a selection of cassette tapes] and I am going to play one now," and as I walked towards the record deck, I had this wonderful feeling of peace sweep over me from behind. And I remember thinking, My God, it's true there really is another life.'

As we can see in almost all of these instances, reassurance has been provided which is then interpreted by the recipient that the deceased is indeed watching over them and their wellbeing. One could argue that this sort of reassurance could have been provided by a counsellor over a period of time, or that time alone would have brought the recipient of the experience to the same conclusion. The important aspect of these experiences is that it was the deceased loved ones themselves that appear to have returned to do this job in aiding the healing process for their survivors.

4

Symbolism and Signs

'There are only two ways to live your life.
One is as though nothing is a miracle.
The other is as though everything is a miracle'

Albert Einstein

NOT ALL ADCS ARE visions, voices or scents – some are more subtle. The bereaved frequently wish or will a higher power, the universe, or their deceased loved one for a sign that he or she still exists and, indeed, that they are all right. Many receive such a sign, though it may take some time to arrive. Occasionally, these signs are so subtle that they may be missed, or they may be discounted as mere 'coincidences'.

Messages are also believed to be conveyed through dreams and natural symbols: rainbows, butterflies, birds and animals, or through the unexpected movement of physical objects. Any of these inexplicable happenings may occur shortly after the death of the loved one or months or years later.

General Signs
Many people wrote of receiving indications that their loved ones were OK. One contributor wrote:

'My brother passed two months ago and we have received various signs that his spirit is still with us. Children in the family have said they have seen him and indeed been caught talking to "him", although no adult could see anyone there. We have had electrical surges in the house, clocks stopping at the time he took his last breath (even electronic digital clocks sticking on 23.02). Picture frames containing him have moved around the sideboard. Others think this is all very weird but I accept it – I believe it is his way of saying he is still with us now.'

Barbra Streisand says her inspiration for the movie *Yentl* came from her father, who spoke to her from beyond the grave. Her father died when she was 15 months old, but she claims to have received two messages from her father in 1979, four years before *Yentl* was released:

> 'The first one was "Sorry", which was astounding because I was angry at him for leaving me,' she said. 'The second message was "Sing proud". I know it sounds crazy, but it was my father telling me to have the courage of my convictions. I made *Yentl*. And I did sing proud.'

At the time, Streisand said she was trying to decide whether to direct and star in *Yentl*, a story of a Jewish girl who disguises herself as her dead brother Anshel so she can study to become a rabbi. A few days before, she made her first visit to her father's grave, which was next to that of a man named Anchel. She adds, 'To me, this was a sign that I should make this movie.'[27]

The death of Kate Boydell's husband Charlie has prompted her to write a survival guide for other young woman who suddenly find themselves widowed. This is available on her own website www.merrywidow.me.uk. She told me:

'Charlie died in very dramatic circumstances; his death was a complete shock to me, but we had been so close as a couple that I knew that even in death he would never be too far away. On the night that he died, when I at last got into bed, I was talking to him in my head, and trying to get him to tell me if he was all right, and if he was happy. All I cared about was whether he was happy.

'I had to know. I asked him to give me a sign, by making some sort of noise. My house is very old, and I often hear creaks and groans, so I listened for a sound, and when I heard nothing but the usual grumbling of tired timber on old stone walls, I said in my head, "That's no good, Charlie, I need to hear a really loud noise – I need to know if you are happy." And then suddenly I head a really loud bang, inside the bedroom, from the direction of his chest of drawers ... and I had my answer.

'When I got up the next morning, I noticed a book had been pulled out of our bookcase, so that it was sticking out from the others around it. It was one of the last books that Charlie read before he died.'

Many letters outlined car registration plates, till receipts, tickets and other day-to-day things seemingly giving them signs. Chris Terry, for example, wrote that his father-in-law, Alfred Evers, died on Good Friday (the 13th) 2001 aged 80 years old and appears to manipulate the sightings of car numbers:

The first one we noticed was KAM 1 – Cammy was the name of the McMillan nurse involved with his care in the hospital a day or so before he died. The next eye-opener was when Vicky (my wife) came home to say she had seen V8 DAD – I had just removed his last can of V8 vegetable juice and placed it on top of his fridge about four months after his death.

'For Christmas 2001, I received a taped book for my car – *Bravo Two Zero* – from Alfred's other daughter. On listening to it, whilst travelling up the M6, I had just got to the bit where the troops were suffering radio (RT) problems when a big 4x4 overtook me at about 100mph – its number was B20 RT!

'Other numbers have been T5 ALF – he collected 5p pieces! P5 BUY, V7 ALF. Vicki has seen ALF and PEG in the same location. Peggy was Alf's wife who died in 1974.

'We bought a new car for our daughter; the reg was VTW (Victoria Terry) but the trade plates casually thrown on the seat for the test drive read AE 080 ... Alfred Evans who died aged 80. Coincidences or not?!'

Another letter described how inanimate objects apparently began to send messages:

'Years later [after the death], whilst baking and playing Def Leppard's "Two Steps Behind", I got a very strong sense that he was there in the kitchen with me. When the cooker buzzer went off and I stooped down to get the cake out of the oven, my necklace came off. The clasp itself was a hard one to unfasten and I laughed and said out loud, "Mark, if that is you give me another sign." Almost simultaneously, his photo that had been hanging in the lounge crashed to the floor (there was no one else in the room) and my son Tom upstairs shouted to tell me that a bird had come into his bedroom. This confirmed it.'

Butterflies

Butterflies crop up again and again in ADCs and I had not realised the close relationship they had with death. Perhaps because of their metamorphosis from an earth-bound caterpillar to a stunning airborne butterfly they are used as a symbol for personal growth and spiritual rebirth and have more recently been seen as a spiritual symbol for life after death. Just walk into any nursery, hospice or hospital and you will find pictures of butterflies. This symbol is also used extensively by many grief counsellors, spiritual and religious centres, and support groups for the bereaved.[28]

One well-documented account is of Bill Rosenberg,[29] who described how, as the casket containing the body of his wife, Julie, was being lowered into the ground at the cemetery, a huge yellow butterfly flew up from the bottom of the grave. It flew over to Bill, then passed by several other family members, resulting in each of them feeling uplifted by their special experience.

Dawn McCoy-Ullrich wrote about her father-in-law who passed away in September 1989:

> 'My husband and I, along with his sister and brother, were all camping on the Father's Day weekend the following year. We were moping around talking about Papa and how much we missed him. In the afternoon, we all retired to our tents for a nap. When we woke up, the entire sky and ground around us were covered with yellow-and-black butterflies. There were literally hundreds of butterflies. It was positively ethereal, as if we were not on earth but somewhere else. This was an incredibly spiritual experience for us and, for years after, we often wondered why this happened. Were the butterflies a sign?'[30]

Another instance concerned a lady who lived all her life in a village in Kent where she became a devoted servant of her parish church and neighbouring churches, and where she was the organist. A few years ago this lady died, having previously assured her friends that when her time came, she would return as a butterfly. At her funeral, everyone noticed that during the vicar's eulogy there was a butterfly in the church, fluttering near, and it later disappeared. Much later at a neighbouring church where this lady used to play, a butterfly appeared as well. The organist used to take special pride in her organ, which is a fairly old and not too reliable harmonium that one has to pedal. She would always insist that fresh flowers were placed upon a special stand nearby at services. To this day, the organ remains temperamental. Yet now it always works when fresh flowers are placed upon the stand, and on three recent occasions has broken down when they are not, leaving the service to continue without it.

A friend told me about an experience which happened at a funeral she attended:

'Hilda reminded me for all the world of the character in the children's book *Mrs Pepperpot*. Her tiny frame and crab-apple cheeks made one smile and, although her face was creased with age, her eyes still twinkled. At the age of 92, she told me that she was "ready to go" and had all the funeral arrangements organised, even down to the food the mourners would eat. She stood at only 4ft 10in tall and yet was strong in the body and mind, having worked hard all her life and brought up her family alone after the early death of her husband. Here she was in the twilight of her years, as strong-minded and cheerful as ever, ready to fly to the next world, as she put it.

'Eventually, she began to grow weaker and was confined to bed for only a short time before she died in her sleep. The day of her funeral would have an atmosphere of celebrating her life rather than mourning. It was a cold, sunny November day when Hilda's tiny, flower-laden coffin was carried into the beautiful old church. The church was chilly and, as the sun was behind the clouds, the mourners shivered a little. The vicar had known Hilda well and spoke of their long association and how cheerful and welcoming she had always been. It was a beautiful service which culminated with words from the vicar who said that he was sure that, at that moment in time, Hilda's soul was on its way to heaven. At precisely that moment, the sun broke through the clouds and poured through the stained glass window directly on to the little coffin. It directed its beam like a spotlight. From the depth of the flowers resting on the coffin, something stirred and a huge, beautiful moth flew directly up inside the ray of light. It was one of those symbolic moments that stay in the memory for ever.'

Joan Silberglied lost her younger brother Robert in the Air Florida Flight 90 tragedy which clipped the Fourteenth Bridge and plunged into the icy waters of Washington's Potomac River, leaving just five survivors. Twenty-one years on, Jean remembers:

'On the day of his funeral, I went outside my parents' condo for a cigarette. The grounds were almost desolate, but as I sat there a small yellow butterfly came up out of nowhere and hit me in my face. As it fluttered away, these words formed in my mind – "Bye, Bob."'[31]

After his 18-year-old son Matt died very suddenly of bacterial meningitis, Bob Pano's daughter Penny had a symbolic ADC with a monarch butterfly, which landed and stayed on her fingers for nearly half-an-hour. Later, Penny found a colour photograph of a monarch which Matt had given her before he died and had handwritten his name on the back of it. These two experiences have helped this bereaved family enormously.[32]

Similarly, in August 1999, when another boxer bitch of Barbara Gilberts' died, she told me:

'I saw her spirit leave her body. The only way I can describe it, it looked like a white butterfly with its wings closed.

'One night last year, I was in bed watching TV (it was late, so it was dark) ... I saw a white butterfly outside my bedroom window. It was Rummie (that was her name) come to let me know she was all right.'

Finally, Roger Butler's letter read:

'I would like to relate two experiences I had – one following the death of my wife and the first experience about seven days before her death, on each occasion concerning the appearance of a red admiral butterfly.

'My wife was terminally ill and, seven days before her death, whilst I was sitting with her at the hospital bed, the window above her head was open about 6in and in fluttered the butterfly, circled the head of her bed, flew out of the window and then returned and repeated its performance ... this was late October 1997.

'The second experience occurred two months following her death in mid-February 1998. I was tending to her grave in our local churchyard and the exact experience happened again. This red admiral butterfly quite suddenly appeared, fluttered around her grave, it then fluttered off and returned about two seconds later and again circled the grave and completely disappeared.

'Certainly, on the second occasion I could not really believe a butterfly would be out on a cold February afternoon!'

Wind or Forceful Energy

Some signs are less than subtle. Dorothy Simpson's story begins with her father dying:

'The minister was saying the prayers when this wind came right through the church, up and over the back of

me. It did it again once more ... everybody was looking
to see where it was coming from.'

When Laura Rebel's brother-in-law passed, she was with him:

'When he took his last breath, I was pushed out of the
room by some energy or other.'

In addition to this mysterious energy being experienced as an
external force being applied somehow to the recipient, in the
form of a push or surge which takes them by surprise, there is even
evidence that, on occasions, recipients can be 'energised' and
given a lift when they most need it.

In the first weeks after her husband's death, Kate Boydell was
totally exhausted, both mentally and physically:

'I wasn't eating properly and I was drained of all
strength. By day, I was trying to cope with the reality of
my situation and, by night, I was trying to find some
respite from it in sleep. But I could not sleep.

'It was during this time that I experienced something
for which I have no rational explanation. As I lay in bed
at night, I became aware of a presence in the room. I
didn't see a bright light, or a shining angel, but I felt
something was with me. And then I felt a surge of
energy flowing into me, just as if I was being charged up
like a battery. I was flat, it's true to say, but in the
morning I felt a new resolve to face what fate had dealt
me, and a kind of inner strength and benevolence that I
found very difficult to explain. I was "charged up" on
maybe half-a-dozen separate occasions – it happened
only in the early months and has not happened since. I
don't know to this day what it was, but I feel that I was
being given the strength to carry on, at a time when I
was at my very weakest.'

The Appearance of Objects

An 'apport' is an object created by mediums and poltergeists, which materialises out of thin air and takes solid form. Most are small objects like coins and jewellery, but larger objects like books and newspapers have been reported. The Scole Experiment Group[33] has had tremendous success with apportation, as the 'spiritual scientists' (deceased humans working from the afterlife to achieve contact with the living) wove energy into matter to produce extremely rare artefacts during their sessions.

The occurrence of apports from the spirit world during séances are both well known and documented, but spontaneous, one-off happenings are apparently less so. Margaret Henderson's husband, for example, died a little while ago and, since that time, she and her daughters have had a number of things happen:

> 'It seems to us like he is trying to make contact. I have never believed in the dead being able to make contact, but I do now.
>
> 'As an example of what happened, on the morning after John died, I opened the back door and there on the mat was a fuschia head, John's favourite summer flower. As I stepped out to pick it up, there was a line of fuschias leading to the window of the room where I work. We do not have a fuschia bush in the garden.'

Taylor Caldwell is a popular novelist. She had a symbolic ADC which is recounted in *The Search For A Soul – Taylor Caldwell's Psychic Lives* by Jess Stearn. Before he died, her husband of 40 years, Marcus Reback, promised to give her a sign. Three days after his death, a shrub of Resurrection Lilies in their backyard bloomed for the first time since it was planted 21 years earlier. Eighteen buds burst open, giving off a joyous fragrance.

A rose was also the centre of another ADC. Robert J. Grant, a hospice volunteer, chronicles his relationship with David, a young patient dying of AIDS who was assigned to him, in his book *Love*

& Roses From David. Rob was given a very large rose from David's garden, but surprisingly it had no scent. The very next day David died and the rose filled the entire house with its aroma. Both Rob and his mother believe it was a sign from David letting them know he was OK.

Cheryl Landon – the daughter of Michael Landon, who achieved fame in the *Little House on the Prairie* TV series – says her beloved dad is guiding her from beyond the grave and she is fulfilling his deathbed wish of helping families throughout America:

> 'My dad and I always had a special bond – and a sense of communication that went far beyond the ordinary, defying explanation,'

43-year-old Cheryl has revealed. 'It continues even to this day as he still guides me from heaven.'

Cheryl travels the country lecturing on issues ranging from ecology to family problems, using film clips from his *Little House* series to illustrate her points. The eldest daughter of Landon's nine children, Cheryl developed a very special telepathic bond with the *Highway to Heaven* star when he saved her life following a car crash. And after Michael's death from pancreatic cancer in July 1991, Cheryl wrote a book about her devoted dad. But when Cheryl was asked to do TV shows to promote it, she admits, 'I was terrified.' Her late dad came to the rescue:

> 'I was home alone and I prayed. I told my dad I was scared. I was awake when he came to me. I heard his voice clearly.'

Michael told her to be confident, and he promised, 'Before you do that first show, I am going to leave you a long-stemmed red rose.'

A month later, a very nervous Cheryl was in a New York hotel room getting ready to appear on *Geraldo*. Suddenly, she recalled:

> 'I heard my dad speaking to me again. "Cheryl," he said, "I want you to go to the fountain in Central Park."
>
> 'I'd never been in New York's Central Park before but, when I got there, I seemed to know exactly where to go. I walked to the fountain. I looked down and saw a long-stemmed red rose! Then I looked up and saw an inscription on the fountain. I was standing at the fountain of Michael the Archangel!
>
> 'I cried without shame and clutched the rose – affirmation that my father was still with me and guiding me.'

Cheryl went on the show with a renewed confidence, started lecturing and began the groundwork for The Landon Center, which uses educational resources and a positive-thinking philosophy to improve people's lives. 'Dad was always there for me,' Cheryl disclosed. And she'll never forget how he saved her life when she was 19. A drunken driver had smashed into a Volkswagen Beetle in which she was a passenger. The bone-crushing 80mph impact killed the other three passengers:

> 'The doctors told Dad I would not survive and that he was wasting his time talking to me

because I was in a deep coma,' she recalled. 'But Dad would not give up. For three days he kept a vigil beside my bed. "Fight, baby, fight," he repeated over and over.

'I remember aching to go toward a light, a brilliant white light ahead of me. And I would have gone, too, I know it. But there was that sound pulling me back: "Fight, baby, fight. Fight, baby, fight."

'When I regained consciousness after three days, they called it a miracle. My father had willed me to live.

'Much later, at the end of his life, I found out that Dad had made a promise to God while I was in a coma. He said, "I promised God that if He would let Cheryl live, I would do something to make the world a little better."

'Twenty-one years after Dad made his promise, I was at his bedside. The doctors had told him he had only three weeks to live. He said, "You know, Cheryl, I cannot die. Society is destroying itself. Our children are in trouble. I can make a difference." Right then and there I made a commitment to my dad that I would carry on his message of love and concern for society. I vowed I would do what I could to help heal our world.'[34]

Barbara Lazear Ascher chronicles her grief following the death of her 31-year-old brother, Bobby, of complications from AIDS in her exquisite book *Landscape Without Gravity*. On the first anniversary of his death, she and her husband, Bob, are sitting on a bench beneath a chokecherry tree where her brother's ashes are buried. Suddenly, a vibrant, garish kite flies towards their faces, before it rises over their heads and disappears in the distance.

But no string is attached to the kite, no one is controlling it. Remembering Bobby's humour and playfulness, they turn to each other, simultaneously exclaiming, 'Bobby! That was Bobby!' as they laugh and cry and hold each other tightly.

David Morrell is best-known as an author, and for creating the movie character John Rambo. His book *Fireflies* narrates the struggle of his 15-year old son, Matthew, who dies of complications during cancer therapy. David sees 'a swirling cluster' of small lights, one of which is Matthew, and they communicate with each other twice. Interesting to this chapter here though is a symbolic ADC he had with a dove that occured during his son's funeral.

Clocks Stopping

Clocks stopping at meaningful times after the death has been well-documented. Wendy A's[35] mother died last year. Having been sick for a while, she knew she was going to die. As Wendy describes:

> 'She wrote me a letter a week or so before she died – in the letter she said, 'you will need a mother for many years to come – I WILL ALWAYS BE THERE.' She said she would try to 'get through' if she could. She died around 5.00pm (I was with her). I immediately left the hospital and came home. Around 7.00pm I was lying on the couch; no one else was home. I was awake but very tired/exhausted and devastated. I felt her move through me. That is the best way I can describe it. I did not physically feel her touch me, I just felt her love. I knew she was 'hugging me' and trying to comfort me. It was kind of a tingly good loving feeling. That was my first experience – one of three times I've had that same feeling.'

It was after this she began to have several symbolic ADC's, perhaps the most profound involving clocks:

> 'When I was cleaning out Mom's apartment one day I commented to my cousin that there was not a clock anywhere in the house — we had moved out almost everything and the phone had been disconnected. I was concerned because I had to be home at a certain time. My cousin left and I was finishing up a few things. I walked by the spare bedroom and heard a clock ticking very loudly. I went in the room and there was a clock that had definitely been in the room before but I could have sworn it wasn't running or ticking prior to that. I still don't know if it was ticking before that or if it just got louder or what, but I had been in and out of that room a thousand times and never noticed it before. It would have been just like Mom to point out the clock so I wouldn't be late for my son's baseball game that day!! This clock has become the primary object associated with my experiences. It runs on a single AA battery.
>
> 'The clock continued to run — I brought it home in July. I put it where it was out of the way but I could check on it. I was very curious to see when it would stop. I was pregnant when Mom died and of course I was upset that she would never see her first granddaughter. I wanted to take the clock to the hospital with me to see if anything happened. I did not take it but I have since noticed that the clock/date on my camera stopped working between the first picture ever taken of my daughter minutes after she was born and the second picture we took. The date is on the first picture but not the second (you cannot accidentally turn it off, you have to stick a pen or something into a hole and manually change it). It could not have been

bumped. I gave my husband an interrogation, he did not touch the date thing between pictures, 'Why would he?' The picture is interesting too – the baby is all lit up but the surroundings are dark. The next picture is completely normal, lit up in a bright hospital room. I had to fix the date later once I realised it had mysteriously been turned off. I think Mom was letting me know she was there.

'Anyway, back to the clock. It ran until sometime around this past Thanksgiving. I'm not sure exactly when it stopped but sometime in November 2002 it stopped at 8.25 (big hand on the five – little hand on the eight) – my mom died 5/8. It crossed my mind that that was odd – but I dismissed it.

'We put up our Christmas tree on 15 December and it was horrible. Probably the saddest night of my life. I had some of Mom's Christmas stuff and was going through everything – sad. That night before I went to sleep I asked Mom to please come to me in another dream (yes, I've had several very interesting dreams also). I was crying and very upset. I wanted and needed her badly. The next morning I woke up, no dream. Before my husband left to do some shopping I showed him the clock. I said, 'Look, Hon, the clock finally stopped at 8.25.' I'm not sure why I decided to show him then because it had been stopped for a while, but I did and he saw that it was stopped.

'About half an hour later I put my 20-month-old son down for a nap. He had been up there for a while just talking and talking for a long time (it's common for him to talk and "read" his books for a while before he goes to sleep) but this was a long time. I went to the bottom of the stairs to check on him and I heard him say, "Grandma … Funny" and he started cracking up laughing. I started getting that tingly feeling I had the day Mom died and something told me to come check the clock. I did and it was ticking again!!

I stood here in my kitchen looking at the clock crying. I felt her move through me again. She was here to comfort me again, I know it. The time never changed but that clock ticked (the second hand moved half a second forward an half a second back until 2 January 2003. I think she was letting me know she was here with me through the holidays. It started ticking again on 01/04/03 and is still ticking but the time is not changing – I'm waiting to see what, if anything, else happens with that. There was a broken clock that chimed right after my grandfather died [as well] – it was a "sign" that the family has talked about over the years.'

Another story involves the neighbour of a friend of mine who was given a clock as a wedding present many years ago. She never liked this clock and it never really worked very well, so it was put to one side in a bedroom. A few years ago, her husband died from a heart-attack while driving home one Sunday lunchtime. To her disbelief and amazement, the clock, for no reason at all, suddenly started to work after 20 years of just sitting on a shelf.

A similar account was sent to me by Claudia Harrison who recounted how she had been given a family heirloom of an ornate grandfather clock which has never worked despite having several people out to try and put it right. It was left on display in their grand hallway as it was such a beautiful item of furniture. However, the night her mother died, after putting the receiver down from hearing the terrible news, the clock whirred into action, chiming beautifully for the first time, she guessed, in over 50 years. She adds, 'It is still ticking and keeping good time to this day.'

Sally Jones wrote:

'The night I returned home after my 37-year-old husband

had died, I noticed that two of the clocks had stopped at 3.45 – the time of his death.' Similarly, Mary-Anne described how 'a clock that we used a lot stopped at 9.25 – we think this was the time we left the hospital after he died – but continued ticking.'

Electricity and Lights

Lights dimming, bulbs blowing and power surges have all been linked to contact from the spirit world, not surprising considering spirits are energy themselves. Steve[36] has had many ADCs from his wife with specific timing involving electricity and lights.

'On a number of occasions over the nine weeks after she died the lighting circuit breaker would trip off when we switched a light on. This never happened before her death, and the house was professionally re-wired three years before she died. On each of these occasions we (my son and I) knew that it was my wife giving us a sign. On the date given, at about 23.30, I stood in the bathroom quietly talking to my wife, and thanking her for all the signs she had given us. Suddenly the whole house went into darkness. I initially thought we'd had a full power cut, but realised that the main ON/OFF switch for the house had turned itself off. After a minute or two, once we'd realised what had happened, we switched it back on again. My son said that we'd better reset both his electric alarm clock, and my own. When we went in to his bedroom, his clock had retained the time, and not reset to 00.00 as it would have been expected to have done. There wasn't a back-up battery fitted in the clock either. My son's alarm clock was my wife's, and the clock as described is now in his bedroom. My wife was in his bedroom changing bed sheets when her haemorrhage occurred.

'On 15 October 2002, I had been talking during

the evening to a number of people at a social club about signs from the other side. When I went to bed that evening, I put our bedroom light on (it's a normal ON/OFF switch), immediately it flickered a little, it dimmed slightly, then got brighter a couple of times. I said, 'Come on love, show us what you can do.' Over a period of about 30 seconds, the light bulb gradually grew dimmer and dimmer as if someone was turning down a dimmer switch. The room eventually finished up in total darkness. I immediately turned on a light in another room, and that light was fine. I later checked the bedroom bulb in another room and found it didn't work any more. I have spoken to many people since about this, including an electrician, and all have never known a light bulb to burn itself out over nearly a minute.'

In November 1996, Lindsay Cannon had just returned home from East Birmingham Hospital:

'My mother unexpectedly passed away there at four o'clock that afternoon and, as you can imagine, my father and I and the rest of our family were in total shock. Within a short time of arriving back home, my daughter Kim asked me for a new light bulb for her bedroom as the old one had just 'blown up'. No problem, but over the next two hours another five or maybe six other light bulbs had blown. Within 24 hours, I had replaced 11 light bulbs around the house. Strange, considering I only ever seem to change one or two every now and again.'

Another contributor commented on similar unexplained phenomena:

'I began to notice that light bulbs were burning out more often – as soon as I changed them, they would blow again. Thinking it may be a faulty batch, I took them

back and exchanged them for another brand, but the
same thing happened again and has done for the last
three years.'

Carol Anderson also reported 'strange things happening with
the lights':

'I have dimmer switches and presumed they were playing
up – lights would dim for no reason or suddenly turn up
to the maximum brightness. The light upstairs which had
regular switches would turn on or off. Obviously, now
living alone I was concerned for safety and, thinking it
was the wiring, I called out several electricians, but none
could find anything to explain it.'

Indeed, to many people, there are other plausible explanations for
such occurrences but to the people it has happened to these
experiences go beyond everyday goings on. Some believe the soul
is able to manipulate things from the hereafter to get your
attention. Often these things are so bizarre and extraordinary that
they do catch the eye, be it clocks stopping at significant times,
strangely behaved butterflies out of season and surges of wind or
strange objects turning up out of the blue. To the bereaved, these
unusual happenings do not seem to be typical and immediately
they are connected to their loved one providing some kind of sign
that they are OK and still with them now.

These phenomena could be interpreted as the natural
occurrences of everyday life which, to the yearning soul, appear to
have mystical significance. Once again, the interesting factor is that
they all occur with apparent spontaneity at the very precise time
that the soul has sought the comfort. How much more convincing
would be some cataclysmic and mystical event? Yet is the wisdom
of the spirits that we could not cope with such an experience and
are more comforted by something small yet deeply significant?

5

REUNIONS
OUT OF THE BLUE

'This life's dim windows of the soul
Distorts the heavens from pole to pole
And leads you to believe a lie
When you see with, not thro', the eye'

WILLIAM BLAKE

WHILE SOME SPONTANEOUS APPEARANCES were seemingly to impart a message or warning or to give guidance, these accounts seemingly had no real purpose. These people did not ask for an experience nor did they expect one, it just came, quite literally, out of the blue.

Bedtime Visions
Fran Bowers was lying in bed one night:

'It was quite stormy outside and electrically charged. I woke up and glanced around the room ... aware of his presence. I turned and he was standing to the side of the bed by the door (the opposite to my side) with his back against the wall; he looked relaxed and happy. I was transfixed and stood watching him for a while, examining his features. He was as real as looking at [my husband] lying next to me. I turned to put on my bedside light but, on turning back, he'd gone. It was just horrendous. I searched all over the house but he'd gone.'

Another experience in the night was reported by Maurice Watkinson:

'I was lying on my right side with my back towards the window. I remember something woke me up and I turned towards the window. To my surprise, I saw someone stood by the window, looking out into the garden. My first thought was how could anyone get into the house – each outside door has more than one lock, this also applies to the windows – but then I realised it was my wife standing there, as she often did. As I looked and was going to speak, she turned towards me and slowly disappeared. From that moment I found I was at peace, and no longer felt so alone. I have no doubt that, when I eventually die, I shall be with her again, and this helps keep me going.'

Heather Davies went out on a Saturday evening with her husband to a local hotel for dinner:

'He dropped dead and this was a terrible shock. When they emptied his pockets at the hospital, I was given his car keys and I had to go and fetch the car we had left in the hotel car park earlier. It was all an awful shock for me – when I came home he had left a jacket hanging on the back of the chair, his toothbrush was still wet, his hairs in his hairbrush, an awful shock.

'The third night after his death and before the funeral, I had been out with two friends who had also suffered losses in the past. I kept saying that, if only I knew he was safe, I could pick up the pieces and carry on. I just wanted to know he was all right.

'My teenage children were asleep in bed, it was 3.33 in

the early morning and I could not sleep. I was sat bolt upright in bed and not the slightest bit sleepy. I remembered that I had a psychic aunt and grandmother and I wondered whether I had any of the same gifts. I thought I would try. I thought, They say heaven is up there, so I cast my mind up to the ceiling and gave every bit of psychic energy I could muster and I grasped out and drew in seeking my husband. It was instant. The room lit up – part ceiling and part top of the wall, the rest of the room was in darkness and the edge between the two swirly mist. It was an upright oblong with the edges rounded. There was the most beautiful man in white robes, holy and saintly and he said in a lovely voice, "He wants to speak with you," and he glided to one side and the last thing I saw of him was the cuff of his sleeve which was pointed. As he glided to one side, there was my husband stood behind him looking really well, not dreadful as he had been looking in the ambulance on the dreaded night, but really rested and well. I felt I hadn't got long and said, "Derek, are you all right?" and he said to me reassuringly, "I'm all right," and then it was all gone.

'I felt enormously privileged. I was then able to sleep and slowly I rebuilt my life. I felt that my husband had asked for permission to come and put my mind at ease that he was all right ... I don't think he could go until then. I felt like he was going on a journey.'

Miss Brown was just eight-and-a-half years old when her mother died very suddenly aged just 34:

'I vividly remember going to bed and my mother stood at the bottom of the bed, dressed as an angel in white with wings. I was a nervous child and felt frightened, I pulled the sheet over my head and, when I pulled it back, she had gone.

'When I told my family about the angel appearing, they said, "You've been dreaming." I don't really know if I had been to sleep or not. I have faith and believe it did happen.'

Mr Bird's father experienced a similar occurrence after the death of his wife in 1982:

'My father chose then to live alone in the house of my childhood. He was a very practical and level-headed man and it was only for the latter years that he moved to my own home, under our care, prior to his demise in 1994.

'I suppose it was some months after my mother had died when he awoke to see her. My father's explanation, as best as I can recall, was that she was her normal height and dressed from head to foot in a long, shining gown. Her arms were by her side but partly open towards him. She had angel-shaped wings which were folded and still. The complete image was on the far side of the bedroom and she was floating between the floor and the ceiling.

'My father's feeling was that his wife had returned in silence, to reassure him that all was well. Having done so, she faded and was gone. I am positive my father never fully accepted my explanation that he had awoken from a wishful dream.'

Lynn Bovis's mother had an experience 34 years ago which, to this day, she cannot offer a reason for:

'No one was ill or anything like that ... My mum was in bed, Dad was asleep beside her. She was thanking God for the safe delivery of my brother David who was asleep in his cot to the right of my mum. David had been born a few days earlier. His cot was in a little alcove.

'Mum said it was a full moon and the bedroom was

fairly well lit. All of a sudden, the two female forms appeared in the alcove next to the cot. One of the women came and sat on my mum's bed. She was a bit older than the other one and wore her hair up in a bun. The younger one was stood next to the cot, bending over it, looking at David and smiling. She had her hair down one shoulder.

'Both of the figures shone like a candle flame. They wore simple, long gowns. The woman who was sat next to Mum put her hand on to Mum's hand; with this, Mum pulled her hand away. Both women then disappeared. The incident lasted about two minutes and Mum said she was both frightened and fascinated.

'No explanation has been given. Mum asked priests and psychics but the only theory to have any belief is the fact that Mum lost two sisters – both died as babies, a few years apart. My mum has never seen the figures since. Her story has never changed and she says what happened is as vivid today as it was then.'

Reunions around the House

Other encounters happen around the recipient's home, as it did when Eileen Redmond's mother died on Christmas Eve 1985:

'For months afterwards, every day I cried ... even out shopping I would see something that reminded me of her and I would burst into tears. I was devastated. One day, my three kids were driving me mad so I went into the sitting room and closed the door to get a bit of peace. I sat on the couch and closed my eyes. Just a few minutes later, my mum stood in front of me with the happiest smile I had ever seen on her face. I opened my eyes to speak to her; just then, my 13-year-old son came bursting in and my mum was gone. I couldn't believe it. I was only in the room a few minutes. If I had been there any longer, I would have said I must have fallen asleep and was dreaming. But what my son said when he saw me convinced me. He said, "Mum, what's wrong? Your face is snow white."

'I knew then that I hadn't imagined it ... my mum came back to tell me to stop crying, that she was happy, and from that moment I stopped crying. It helped me so much.'

Following a lengthy illness, Margaret Barber's mother died in July 1995:

'A week later, at around 10.00pm, while washing dishes in the kitchen, I heard muffled noises in the hall behind me. I was alone in the house at this time but felt no fear as I knew it was my mother. I never saw her but felt her presence instantly. I walked into the hall and said, "It's all right, Mum ... we're all OK ... you can go now." The "presence" faded and I knew she had gone for ever.'

Vianne Roberts's gran and grampy were taken in the same year within a few months of each other. In the summer of that year, all the loose ends over their flat were tied up:

'Because my sister and brother had lost our mother, we took some of the share of the money due. On the morning I got the cheque, I was reading the share-out details at the table in my sitting room in my flat. I looked towards the door and in the hallway I saw my gran walk across the hallway – she was quite bent and had a smile on her face and was wearing clothing I remember her in. Gran was as solid as you or I and, being probably only about 2ft away from her, I could not only see her properly but could have touched her ...

'A few months after that, the second one happened. I got up at around midnight unable to sleep and sat in the chair in the corner of the room with the TV off. By the table were chairs, one being by the door. I was calm in myself; I sat there for an hour or so every night for about a month and, each time I looked at the TV screen, I saw Grampy in the chair that was placed by the door. I would take my eyes away from the TV but I could not see him sitting on the chair that way, only if I looked at the [blank] TV screen. He looked happy and again dressed in clothes I remember.'

Another contributor remembers how their father just 'appeared':

'He said he had just come to visit and he had his slippers on. This was a family joke as my mother was always nagging him about taking his shoes off at the door and wearing his slippers. This was a good way of confirming it was him, even though I could see him.'

Laura Rebel's first ADC experience was when she was 16:

'It was a woman I didn't know ... I was petrified. I told my father about my experience and he used to make a joke of it which used to annoy me. He passed over shortly after and I forgot about my experience until the day my father appeared in front of me, solid and in colour, not see-through. He smiled then disappeared. I think he came back to tell me I wasn't imagining things. That was in 1974.'

Mary Mullally lost her son:

'I loved him so very much ... he was only 34 years old and a ray of sunshine in my life and I am dead inside now, but I have seen him at least four times for a split-second and it was magnificent and I keep wishing it would happen more often. I feel his presence a lot and keep talking to him and looking at a special photo of him.'

Experiences away from Home

Michael Crichton is best known as the author of science fiction books, including *The Andromeda Strain*. Michael describes his father's death in his autobiography, *Travels*, whereby he feels his father's presence at the funeral home, and knows he's there. Michael is equally certain he doesn't sense his father the next day at the funeral home, during the church service, or at the cemetery.

Duncan Dale-Emberton wrote about the appearance of a loved one in a place that meant a great deal to both of them:

> 'I went on holiday to my Dorset home and looked around the family church of the Holy Trinity in Dorchester, which was then Church of England. As I reached the lectern, I was overwhelmingly aware of my father's presence; he had died in 1951, at the age of 36, when I was nine years old, but was certainly there then, all those years later. He had been a lay reader who, when we [the children] were past first infancy, had let us decide whether we still wanted to attend services. I did.'

Sensing a presence is such a common encounter. C. S. Lewis, the scholar, professor and author of more than fifty books on religion, fantasy and science fiction, details his grief as a widower in his journal, *A Grief Observed*. After his wife, Joy, dies of cancer, he has 'an instantaneous, unanswerable impression of her presence,' and experiences 'the impression of her mind'. Earlier in life, he felt 'the ubiquitous presence' of his deceased friend, Charles Williams.

Llewelyn Rhys remembers a family occasion which he feels his dead grandmother just had to attend:

> The only time I actually saw something was on my daughter's wedding day on 6 September 1986. About

halfway through the reception, I suddenly felt very cold and had a strong feeling of wishing to be on my own. I looked up at the north of the marquee, and there was the outline of my grandmother's face. She died in 1946, and clearly had been "allowed back" to see her great-granddaughter married. The whole episode was over in about three seconds.'

Gay Pilgrim told me of a time she was 'visited' by her father about a year after he had died when she was about 12:

'I wasn't a mystical child. Indeed, my mother always opined that if I was in a post office queue and a ghost tried to barge in, I'd tell them smartly to go to the back of the queue! So what follows is quite surprising.

'At the time we were living in a caravan on a farm. I was alone in the caravan doing the washing up. It was late afternoon but, being summertime, perfectly light, the sun was still shining as it started to drop towards the horizon. I can't remember what I was thinking about, but I don't believe I was unhappy or sad. Probably I was hoping that I was doing the washing up OK and my mother wouldn't tell me off! Anyway, I heard and felt (caravans tend to move when someone steps into them) someone come into the van, and without thinking turned to say "Hello, Daddy". I just knew it was him. It would be untruthful to say because it smelled like him, but there was something particular about that sense of his presence. What I can recall vividly, even after all these years, was the shock when I saw there was no one there. The contradiction between my "sense" of who had come in, and the concrete reality of there being nothing, no one, was very confusing. What sense could I make of this? At the time I don't think I did make any sense of it. As I've said, I can still recall the physical shock of the realisation that it wasn't my father. That it would never be my father again. He was dead. Gone. Absent forever. I never mentioned this experience to anyone, and over time forgot about it.

'Later, much later when I had become an adult and recalled this incident, it seemed to me that my father had come to visit me to, quite literally, bring me to my senses. His death had been a terrific trauma for me. My mother and I didn't get on at all well and his death left me emotionally adrift. I have very little memory of this period, but I have learned since that I changed quite considerably after his death, my withdrawal causing my mother serious concern. My father's "visit" shocked me into facing up to and acknowledging his death, thereby allowing me to get on with my own life. Of course, this is only my interpretation of what happened. I am well aware that a psychologist would provide a very different reading. But they weren't there and, believe me, it was absolutely real. I *know* what I experienced, even after all these years.

Hugs

For some, after-death communications are not simply visual or auditory experiences – the reunion with a loved one can often be sensed or experienced physically as well. Sharon wrote to me saying that she remembers her mother's embrace, and the comfort that she derived from it:

'In 1999, I was very down ... I was washing the dishes while looking out of the window at the garden. Only two children live at home and they were chatting in the living room. Suddenly, I felt two arms wrap around my waist and hug me; it felt warm and relaxing. I said, "That feels nice," thinking it was my husband. Then the hairs on the back of my neck stood up when I heard my husband [in the other room] talking with the children. Suddenly but smoothly, the arms slipped away.

'I knew it was my mother – it happened again a few days later but since then I've not seen or felt anything. I was never scared – just relieved my mother was with me.'

Norma waited for contact from her aunt when she passed and thought it would not happen, 'but when I visited her grave I felt her arm around my shoulders'.

When Chris Jones was about 20 he recalls sitting at home one evening, watching television:

'I became aware, I can put it no other way, that I could neither move nor speak, even my eyes seemed frozen. After a few seconds, just as I was beginning to panic, I felt two hands somehow come out of the back of the sofa and gently hold me. At first, I tried to struggle but still could not move, then, very quickly, a feeling of contentment and reassurance spread over me. I have never felt so "held" in my life. After a few more seconds, the hands withdrew as they had come – I could move again.

'The really strange thing, apart from the obvious, is that I knew immediately that the hands were those of my paternal grandfather, a most undemonstrative, even withdrawn, man. I can't remember him ever touching, let alone holding, me in life. He had died some years previously.'

A Stroke or Touch

Michael Landon was a very popular actor, director and writer. He had an ADC with his deceased father[37] while kneeling before his coffin. Michael felt his dad touch his shoulder and heard him say, 'It's OK, kid. Don't worry. I'm fine. Everything is going to be all right.'

Melissa Whitehead awoke one Thursday morning at about 5.30am because she could hear footsteps walking around her bedroom:

'I was pretty scared because my boyfriend and I live together and he was next to me at the time. I opened my eyes but I could see no one ... [yet] I could still hear the footsteps. I cuddled Ray really tight and basically tried to hide behind him because I was really scared. Instinctively, I knew it was Grandmother, but this was the first time I had experienced anything like this. I heard her walk over to the bed and I felt a strange pressure like someone had sat on the bed. Stranger still, they had sat on Ray! Then I felt someone squeezing and gently rubbing my left ear.

'I felt quite tense and eventually felt calmer and began to doze off. About an hour-and-a-half later, at about 7.15am, I awoke again with someone walking around the room and, although I was less afraid, I was still quite nervous. Again, I opened my eyes and saw no one. I kept my eyes open and felt someone sit on the bed, this time right next to me, again gently squeezing and rubbing my left ear. I felt this had some kind of significance so I asked (in my head), "Why are you rubbing my ear?"

'Strangely enough, I didn't need to ask, I already knew ... we had a saying when we were kids about which ear itched and what it meant – right for spite, meaning someone was saying something horrible to you, and left for love, meaning someone was saying they loved you. I believe my grandma was coming through to tell me she loved me. I also found out later from my dad that she was always playing with my ears when I was a baby.'

Dave Rogers wrote about a one-off occurrence which happened just two weeks after his wife's death almost 16 years ago:

'One night, as I lay in bed, I suddenly felt her stroking and touching my hand ... I could feel her there with me though, sadly, I could not see her.'

All of these accounts outline experiences which just 'happened' as the person was going about their daily routine and perhaps at the time not really thinking specifically about the deceased. They were in bed or getting on with their lives be it in their own home or elsewhere. These powerful experiences of just 'seeing' loved ones or, indeed, sensing their touch or hug are all incredibly poignant encounters which leave the recipient totally fulfilled and confident that their loved ones are safe and well.

6

AUDITORY COMMUNICATIONS

'If someone calls you once more, say 'Speak,
Lord, your servant is listening'''

1 SAMUEL 3:9

CARL SAGEN, THE CORNELL University astronomer and author, wrote about his own experience in *Parade* magazine:

'Probably a dozen times since their deaths, I've heard my mother or father, in an ordinary, conversational tone of voice, call my name. They had called my name so often during my life with them. I still miss them so much that it doesn't seem strange to me that my brain occasionally will retrieve a kind of lucid recollection of their voices.'

But can auditory experiences be explained away so easily? How can we explain away voices of the deceased proclaiming news, unveiling things the recipient did not and could not have known? Marilyn Pringle wrote:

'When I was 11 years old, I lost my brother aged 25 ... [he was] unable to talk all his life, only mumbles. I used to teach him to say my name, Marilyn. He tried so hard, but just couldn't get it right. One night, just after he died, I lay awake, I hadn't been to sleep. I was fully aware I heard his voice so clear saying, "Marilyn", so perfect I have never ever forgotten – I am now 52 years old.'

It is as if the dead are determined to prove, beyond any reasonable doubt, the possibilities beyond our own imaginings and understanding. Blind people see deceased loved ones, entities or ghosts, and the deaf are able to hear, as happened to Collette Donoghue.

Collette has been contacted more than once by different loved ones in both dramatic and quite simple ways:

'For example, I hear loved ones, as opposed to seeing them. They've called me by name, for dramatic reasons like warnings, and for no apparent reason at all. I also smell various relatives and friends and then I sense them "there". But one time in particular does haunt me to this day – more so, once you've read part of my history, you will see the bigger picture and then see why ...

'When I was 21, I contracted meningitis and septicaemia and, as a result of that, I have been left half-deaf and, as a consequence, I find it extremely hard to wake up. My family has a hard time trying to rouse me. It's as if I go to sleep so deeply that I lie somewhere between unconscious and comatose!

'My father died. I had been caring for him prior to his death and, although I knew his death was imminent, I was never quite ready emotionally. I was inconsolable and could not come to terms with my loss. I was just crestfallen with grief to say the least ...

'I felt my dad's presence come into the room and, although I loved and still love him dearly, I was terrified. So I moved my two-seater across my front room so that the back of the sofa was in front of his presence (which seems a funny thing to do now, as I put it in writing, as I loved and still love my dad unequivocally). I sat down, and carried on smoking a cigarette.

'At some point after that, I must have fallen asleep while the lit cigarette was still in my hand. I was awakened by a very sombre and angry voice, screeching in my ear – and I quote – "Get up, will you?" in my deceased father's all too familiar south-west Irish accent! And although I knew he was dead and that I was awake and not dreaming, for a split-second I was partially convinced that he was still alive, as I knew the voice to be his without any hesitation. At this point I was upright, fully coherent and traumatised with fear, hoping and praying that I did not get it wrong.

'At which point, I could smell my dad's scent and it was as if he was producing the much-needed proof I had hoped I wasn't wrong about and I realised I could still feel his lips and indentation left on my left earlobe where he had screeched to wake me from my comatose state! His presence behind me was somewhat full and bounding, like how you would perhaps describe a pulse, and that feeling from him did not leave me when I finally extinguished my cigarette. When I sat back into the sofa once again, I noticed a 2in burn area in one of the cushions ... but fortunately it had not set alight.'

Another of Collette's experiences happened not long after her cousin's death:

'I was once again in my front room listening to music on my headphones – I must add that the volume was on the maximum – when I heard my name being called outside of the headphones and from my right to the back of me and it was very distinct and I knew instantaneously that it was my cousin Jason who had died.

'I must state that the fear of God entered me because I could not have heard anyone, being half-deaf. Because previously, whilst listening to music on my headphones, the only way I would know someone was screaming at me was because I could see their lips moving! But on this occasion I knew that there was no person to see, because I knew by the accent, tone and pronunciation of my name – Collette is pronounced as it's written, and the only person who said it differently was my cousin who pronounced it "Clet" – that it could only be Jason calling me, instantaneously!'

Jenny admits that she has anticipated a great deal of cynicism in recounting her experience.

'This communication is hard for people to accept, therefore I have mentioned it only to a couple of friends and my mother.

'I was lying in bed, very early in the morning, about 5.00am. Because I found it hard to sleep following my husband's death, I often had the radio on during the night, usually the World Service. I was thinking of nothing and trying to sleep when the radio sound faded and my husband spoke to me, his voice coming from the radio! He said, "Jenny, are you awake?" I answered, "Yes, I'm awake." He said, "Are you all right?" and I said, "Yes." When I realised I was talking to the radio, I was shocked, surprised and panicking to say the least. My body felt tingly all over as if I had a shivery fever.

'When this happened, the music on the radio faded back in ... It's a very strange situation to be in. I am a level-headed person, not given to talking with someone over the radio! My regret is that, because of my shock, I didn't hear what he said next, although I was aware of him speaking a little more ...'

In 1990, Marlon Brando's son Christian was involved in controversy surrounding the death of Dag Drollet, the lover of Brando's daughter Cheyanne. The American press speculated that Marlon Brando's friends feared he was close to cracking after he told them he was being haunted.

The actor is said to have spoken of sheets mysteriously flying off his bed and 'cold ghostly lips' whispering, 'I should not have died,' in his ear. The actor's former wife said he was convinced it was Dag's spirit. 'It's terrifying,' Brando is said to have admitted. 'I know it's Dag's angry spirit.'[38]

Veronica's mum was in bed asleep when a voice said to her, 'Marianne' – she sat up in bed and saw a whitish mist in the bedroom. 'She said she heard Dad as clear as anything. It woke her up and he said, "Don't worry."'

Lesley Hanafi's mother died peacefully at home after an illness which gradually debilitated her. The pair were extremely close and about four days after she died:

'I was awakened by my telephone ringing at about 6.30am. Although it was February, the room was full of brilliant sunshine. I answered the phone and said, "Hello?" My mother was on the line ... I was amazed and asked her how she was feeling. She said she felt heaps better and felt she had turned a corner. So vivid was this vision that in the back of my mind I was panicking about all the people who were coming to the funeral we were organising and how to cancel caterers ... all sorts of practical worries that would have to be addressed! When our conversation finished, I came to, with the true grey light of a February dawn in the room *and* the telephone receiver in my hand.'

Another lady had similar experiences:

> 'Then I started dreaming about him; I didn't see him
> initially, just talked to him on the phone and felt his
> presence. I never ended a phone call with him by
> replacing the handset – I'd become aware in my dream
> state that I was waking up and would wake up, face wet
> with tears and sobbing because I didn't want to sever the
> contact, the link with him, because I also knew the hard
> reality that was waking when I awoke.'

Linda's sister's friend committed suicide about four years ago:

> 'She had a history of mental illness and conflict. I
> experienced, awake, her voice telling me gently to let
> my sister know that she was happy "now that my soul is
> at peace".'

Other messages are incredibly personal, with words sometimes
so abstract they only make sense to the recipient. Llewelyn
Rhys's experience happened on 3 July 1971 after the funeral of
his Scottish uncle, of whom he was very fond and who had
acted *in loco parentis* – he was his grandmother's younger
brother:

> 'To cut a long story short, I had a curious but strong urge
> to walk to a lake in his grounds after the funeral
> reception. It was a kind of "pulling" feeling. Suddenly I
> swung round and heard my late uncle say, "Are you sure
> you want this to happen?" It was the voice of my uncle
> when he was about 20 years younger. But I did not see
> anything. Somehow, he had been "allowed back" to warn
> his nephew of danger – the warning was heeded and
> never was anyone proved to be so right.'

Sharon Stables lost her 22-year-old son:

> 'He was back-packing with his girlfriend and, while he was in India, he had a brain haemorrhage ... by the time we got him home, we weren't allowed to see him.
>
> 'Since then, we have had all sorts happen, but probably the most interesting would be when I went to bed one night, lay very quietly and tried to contact my son. The whole episode would take too long to write, but briefly I heard my son say, "Mum ... Mum! Are you there?" I then had a conversation with him and finished by saying, "But how do I know I am not having a two-way conversation with myself?" He then told me he was with his friend – who I know and I am in contact with his mum – who told me three things. When I checked with his mum, all three were correct and I couldn't have known anything. Since then, it has happened a couple of times.'

To conclude, it seems such auditory messages are usually short and concise – they could be compared with text messages or telegrams which typically contain around 25 words. They are communicated in the authentic voice of the deceased person, complete with speech impediments, accents and characteristic pronunciations – the voice can be internal or external, as clear as if I were talking to you now.

I have deliberately tried not to refer to specific authorised religions in my writing or quotations but the reason I used the quotation at the head of this chapter is that I wish to liken our current times with the times of the boy Samuel. The story leading up to this quotation begins with the statement 'In those days the word of the Lord was rarely heard and there was no outpouring of vision'. It seems to me that in our increasingly materialistic world our ability to hear the voices imparted to us from the spiritual side of life may be impaired and thus it may be that occasionally, when we are least expecting it, as indeed with Samuel, we possibly become more aware of these things.

7

SCENT FROM ABOVE

*'The truth is sort of mysterious and sometimes
has nothing to do with facts'*

OLIVER SACKS

SMELLING A FLORAL PERFUME, a favourite scent, after-shave or brand of tobacco, or any instantly recognisable smell which can unmistakably be attributed to the deceased, appears to be an extremely common experience. A vision seldom accompanies the smell – or olfactory ADC, to give it its proper name – it is as if the smell says it all. The recipient knows where it is from, who it is from and what it is saying.

Sometimes, this aroma precedes the death, as Cecilia Blackie describes happening before her husband died. 'I was awoken by a lovely fragrance which lasted for a few minutes. It happened again the following night.' She couldn't think what it was, 'but wished it had gone on and on'.

Another lady described how, 'Three days before he died, the house was filled with the scent of his favourite cigars.'

A Scented Passing
Many wrote about the phenomena of smelling flowers in the room at the moment someone passed away – ' an aroma of

flowers at the moment our mother passed away ...' and '... I had a strong scent of lilies when my mother was dying, yet there weren't any flowers there.' Rita King also wrote that, on the death of her father in hospital, and the death of her mother in her own home, she experienced 'an overwhelming scent of flowers on both occasions'.

Jenny Jackson also had this experience when her husband was in hospital terminally ill and unable to communicate:

> 'As I sat by his bed surrounded by drips ... and trying to say goodbye, I became aware of a scent of flowers. I had never actually been present at a death before and asked his nurse if that was usual. She said, "No," but that she could smell it, too. Was it her perfume? It wasn't. We both looked out of the window into a bare concrete yard full of oxygen cylinders – nothing there. I know it wasn't my imagination as she smelled it, too. At that time, I didn't recognise the scent, but in October 1990 I went to see my husband's family in Australia and, in a remote village in Western Australia, I smelled the smell again – it was honeysuckle, my husband's favourite flower for scent. I have always believed that this was his way of saying goodbye to me.'

Lavinia Bradley describes a similar occurrence:

> '[My husband] died with me but, when the undertakers came to take him away, I couldn't bear it and went out into the garden. I didn't come in until they had driven away with him. I went to the empty room and was deluged in a sweet floral scent, almost like an embrace. For an instant, I almost felt this was some sort of last gesture from him, then reasoned I was being ridiculous and that probably undertakers used some sort of freshener. To this day, I have never asked if this is their

practice because, fantastic though it is, I wanted to believe it was something from him.'

Again, after Carol Thomas's mother had suddenly passed away while staying with her for a visit:

'After paramedics, doctors and undertakers had completed their formalities, my father and I went to see her for the last time, laid out on the guest bed. I was immediately struck by a strong "odour" of flowers. It was not really "natural" and I had not smelled it before. I tended to think it was how the body had been prepared. Even when they took her away and after a further two nights when my father slept in there, that same smell pervaded the room – although no one else was particularly aware of it.

'We then decided to take my father back to his house. When we arrived, I needed something out of a case which had been put on the guest bed upstairs. As I opened the door, I was literally knocked backwards by an extremely pungent scent, flower-like, and instinctively said, "Oh, hello, Mum!" The smell was also smelled again in Dad's lounge where Mum used to sit.'

Scent ... to Inform of Death

It is these experiences which are problematic for sceptics who try to explain ADCs as grief-induced hallucinations or hysteria. How can one be grieving for someone they are yet to know they have lost? And the fact that these encounters happen at the exact time a last breath has been taken ... I think you will agree, evidence here points to there being a lot going on in the universe which has yet to be comprehended.

At the time Eric Dyson's mother died in 1947, he was with his father and brother in the living room when they all noticed 'a very heavy, sweet scent of flowers which lasted for only a few moments but was very definite'. His mother was, at the time, very ill in hospital:

> 'She had always told us that she would not have wallflowers (she was very specific about this) in the house as their scent had been noticed before her own mother's death ... I can confirm this as a true account of our experience but have no explanation for it other than a visitation.'

Mr Winepress wrote to describe a similar experience:

> 'On the day my dear wife died, at 5.00am, as I lay in bed, the room was suddenly filled with an overpowering smell of flowers, although there weren't any in the house ... this also happened on the following two nights.'

The same experience is reflected in a separate account:

> 'The day my mother died, and for about three months after her death, I was aware of the same kind of floral perfume in different parts of the house and at different times of day. It did not happen anywhere else.'

Patricia Fountain wrote:

> 'A neighbour of my mother's, her official carer and on whom she depended absolutely, died after a short illness. I woke in the morning, in my own home, and the bedroom was pervaded by what I can only describe as a flowery perfume, or pot pourri. I do not have flowers or other such things in the bedroom. I even asked my husband if he had changed his aftershave. I gave no more thought to it until later that evening when I had a call from the neighbour's son to tell me of his mother's death and asking me to break the news to my mother.'

A friend of Harry Lovelock's was dying from cancer:

> 'I was visiting my daughter in Leicestershire, the weather
> was cold and my bedroom bare of flowers or any kind of
> perfume. I woke at 3.20am aware of a strong, heady,
> pleasing aroma and I sat up, fully awake, switched on my
> bedside lamp and looked around the room, this time
> breathing in deeply in an attempt to ensure that I wasn't
> imagining things. After a time, I lay back feeling
> comforted but unable to explain why.
>
> 'I drove back to London after breakfast and, switching
> on my answering machine, heard the young woman's
> husband say that my friend had died, in the hospice, at
> 3.25 that morning.'

Dr Ernst's wife died on 16 October 1998 after suffering from lung
cancer. He wrote:

> 'We had a truly wonderful marriage for 33 years, of love,
> laughter and total happiness. During the last few
> months, I do not think two people could have been
> closer than we were. We had been able to discuss our
> lives together but, most important of all, we were able to
> say goodbye, and each give our permission for the other
> to let go. We both had faith and were practising
> members of the Church of England. Neither of us were
> psychic, although we often knew what the other was
> thinking. I think this was due to having a close marriage
> with good communication.
>
> 'On the night of 16 October, I went to bed at about
> 10.00pm and fell into a deep sleep. About 3.00am I
> woke up, and the room was full of the scent of roses. I
> called out to see if she was there, but I heard and saw
> nothing. I was at all times totally awake and tried to find
> the source of this wonderful aroma, but there was

nothing in the house or garden remotely like it. The experience lasted about 20 minutes.'

When Margaret's brother died, she, too, 'experienced a wonderful scent throughout the house which was collaborated by friends who came to help and can only be described as "down to earth". The perfume was obvious but so delicate and, in spite of the deep sorrow I felt at Sandy's passing, there was the most wonderful feeling of peace.'

Rosalie Double recalls the day her dear mother died, in 1952:

'I too, experienced an intense scent of fresh flowers – all separate and identifiable. No one else in the family could smell them and, when I realised it could be a message from my mother, it was cut off immediately ... as suddenly as the shutting of a door, as if, once the message of incomparable beauty had got through to me, that was sufficient.'

Scent after Death

The majority of ADCs – by far – occur some time after passing over. For some, this is a matter of weeks or months and, for others, years. However, the following two accounts happened very soon after. In the case of Margaret Kemp-Lewis, it was when driving back from the hospital after her mother had died:

'Suddenly, the car was filled with the sweet scent of flowers and, although I didn't understand why, I knew it had to be connected with her death. It's something I will never forget and I feel very privileged to have had that experience.'

In a similar vein, Mrs Fleming's mother's unexpected death happened back in March 1969:

'Having dashed down from the Welsh border to the New Forest and trying to comfort my father, I felt I would never sleep that night. As I lay in the dark, the most exquisite scent of flowers filled the room – better than hyacinths, lilies or orange blossom, but similar – it really was like nothing I have ever smelled before or since. I felt a great sense of comfort, and fell into a dreamless sleep and woke quite refreshed to face the day.'

Maggy Brook also told me about:

'... a curious incident which occurred when I was 12. My mother died of kidney disease and my father (a devout Christian) arranged for the funeral service to be held in our sitting room. My mother was a Roman Catholic but never ever set foot in a church ...

'The coffin was in the room for two to three days and, afterwards, there was an overpowering smell of spring flowers there, in fact, I would often just go in to smell them. It is only in later years I realise this was a very strange phenomenon – I mean, if I move a pot of hyacinths out of my room the smell won't linger more than a day – how on earth can it stay a year or so?'

After the death of 'a very dear friend', Mrs Cooper entered the bedroom and there was a 'very strong perfume of flowers'. Then, 'a few weeks after my husband passed away, I entered the hall of my flat ... the smell of perfume was terrific. It was quite scary, it happened again but this time was very slight. It really is quite a mystery.'

Soon after the death of one of Oseni Lawal's childhood friends, the 18-year-old Muslim remembers:

'I prayed fervently that he may go to heaven. I prayed alone in an open yard. After a couple of minutes of praying, I sensed a sweet smell of flowers around me of whose origin I could not tell. My belief then was that it was my friend who was present in spirit just to say, "All is well," as if to say, "Your prayer is answered and I am now peacefully at rest in heaven." '

> When Englebert Humperdinck bought Jayne Mansfield's old Hollywood home shortly after her death, he said, 'I'm sure she lived with me in spirit for a time – I'd smell her rose-petal perfume. Once I saw a figure in a long, black dress in front of me. It was Jayne, but it wasn't frightening.'[39]

Mrs Sharman wrote about an experience both she and her daughter had:

'My daughter had a little girl, stillborn. It was after that we both experienced a strong smell of roses in two different rooms in two different houses. This was most strange and, needless to say, I searched the room for evidence of the smell but found nothing. It happened once to us both and is something we will never forget.'

An elderly lady friend of Mrs Marsh had lost her son as a result of a lorry knocking him off his bicycle:

'She said that, following his death, she experienced a beautiful, calming sensation of flowers throughout her bedroom in the middle of the night. She then felt "at peace" and has always felt it could have been a floral "message" of some sort.'

Other olfactory experiences happened years after the passing. Michele Pretty describes:

'I am an only child, Daddy's Girl, or I was until he died when I was nine years old. We were very close when he was alive, he'd only ever wanted a little girl, although I do feel my mother was made to feel slightly jealous as we were always off together.

'I got pregnant at a very young age – 14 – and had a son but he was induced so it wasn't really a natural start to labour. Another son followed two years later, again induced. Some time later, I was pregnant with my daughter and, as the due date was approaching, felt very apprehensive as I hadn't gone into labour naturally and didn't know what to expect. On my due date, I felt very tense and upset because I was waiting for a sign that labour was starting – I didn't realise then that most babies don't arrive on the due date!

'At about 7.30pm I could smell aftershave – it was Brut. As it was just after Christmas, I thought that maybe the boys had got hold of their father's stock of Brut he'd received as Christmas presents. We went to investigate but, no, there was no possible way they could've got to it as it was high up on top of the wardrobe! The funny thing was the smell seemed to be around me, and me only. Everywhere I went in my flat, it followed me! At this point, my husband had goose bumps on his body and felt quite scared – he didn't believe in the afterlife – but all I felt was very calm inside as if someone was somehow invisibly reassuring me.

'After about ten minutes, the smell disappeared and my calm feeling went, too; we were all quite astounded. Six days later, I gave birth, naturally and very easily, to a beautiful daughter. I just wondered if it was my father telling me in his way that there was nothing to be scared of because everything would be OK and I, too, would have a daughter to be proud of!

'I've since gone on to have another son but my father

didn't make an appearance with him. By the way ... when
my father was alive, his favourite aftershave was, yes,
you guessed it, Brut!'

Mrs Archer has '... had the wonderful experience of smelling a
perfume, so beautiful — a real bouquet of flowers. This has
[happened] four times on anniversaries of my mum's death ...'

On three occasions,' Mrs Atkinson has '... had the strong smell
of tobacco and cinnamon which was definitely my dad, but was
never noticed by my husband,' and Jan Simmonds can 'also smell
Victory-V sweets from time to time and my grandmother is the
only person I know who used to eat these — so I think she is still
around me now.'

It is often the case that such experiences happen at the actual
moment of death. This is a well-known and documented
occurrence witnessed by those in the actual presence of the dying
and something to which many nurses and care assistants the world
over can testify. Interestingly, though, I received the same amount
of letters from people who had had this particular type of
encounter at the precise moment of their friend's or relative's
death, but who had not been in their presence at the time.

8

MESSAGES OF HOPE

'Death is the only inescapable, unavoidable, sure thing. We are
sentenced to die the day we're born'

THE FOLLOWING ACCOUNTS ALL occurred at a time
when the recipient was unwell – either in hospital or at home.
Perhaps more than other kinds of ADCs, these were particularly
comforting, since not only was the encounter unexpected but also
happened at a low time when the recipients were feeling especially
alone and frightened. In all cases, the recipient was left feeling
calmed and reassured that, despite their condition, their time had
not yet come.

Hospital Visitors
A corporal in the Royal Army Medical Corps became quite choked
as he described an incident to me which occurred back in 1988. He
was taking part in a military parachute jump called a HALO which
is a high-altitude, low-opening, oxygen-assisted parachute jump.

'I was the second man out of the aircraft and, when I
exited the aircraft, I caught the altimeter on the side of the
fuselage. I thought no more about it and left the aircraft.

Everything was just fine and I was in good line following the guy in front of me ... every so often you check your altimeter to make sure. Because we open at such a low altitude you have a window of 500m – the alarm goes off to let you know you are ready for opening. I looked down at the altimeter and noticed I had actually smashed and broken it so didn't know my rate of descent or things like that. I was only literally ten seconds behind the guy in front of me so I got a bit panicky – I had to worry about what altitude I would open my chute at. I originally thought about opening it straight away and going from a HALO to a freefall but, in the end, I just watched the guy in front of me and, when he started to open, I would pull my 'chute. So I followed the guy down, very nervous.

'Then, all of a sudden, I had a very calming feeling all over me and it was a case of: "There's no problem, you can do this." I was filled with loads of confidence. The guy in front deployed his 'chute at 800m and, by the time I had seen him deploy his 'chute, I had already deployed mine and was about 300m past him travelling at over 100mph ... so I opened up the 'chute, looked up at it fully deployed and then looked down and immediately hit the ground with a tremendous force.

'My recollection ends there. All I know is I came round and was in the military hospital in Cyprus. I'd seriously damaged my back and was in a very bad condition in ICU where I was under observation.

'At one stage, a nurse came into the room and asked me how I was doing. I said, you know, "Fine, OK." It was only my third day of being in the hospital so I was on quite strong painkillers. The nurse asked me who was I talking to, and I said, "Well, I am talking to my grandmother." And she says to me, "Well, there is no one here and you've just had a 40—45-minute conversation with this person in your room."

'Now, I can remember her being there. I could describe every detail, her hair, how she moved, how she breathed, how she smelt and I was talking to her for a great deal of time, talking about the accident and how it happened and at no stage did it enter my head as to why she was there – we were just talking away – it was a great experience. The only problem with it was my gran actually died two years prior to the accident. Despite this, for me to see her at the side of my bed seemed to be the most natural thing in the world – we were very close. At one stage, my parents were in the Army and I actually spent a couple of years living with my grandmother, so we got very close. To see her there at a time of crisis and a time of need ... it was the most calming and awe-inspiring thing I have ever experienced.'

Jack Hunter's late grandfather came to him with a message just when he needed him. Before returning back to base while on leave from the RAF in 1941, he decided to call on his GP. The doctor suggested he attend the Chest Clinic for an X-ray.

'When I was given a complete examination by the consultant, he then told me that I wasn't to concern myself about returning to the RAF as he would be contacting them to inform them that he was sending me to hospital as I had TB.

'Over a year later, still in the City Hospital, Edinburgh, I really started to get worse – I had developed pneumonia and other complications so I was moved into a special small ward. It was during the smallpox epidemic here in Scotland, which started in Aberdeen and no visitors were allowed into the hospital as one of the wards was used for the smallpox patients. I was told years later that a policeman had been sent to my home to warn my father and mother – I wasn't expected to survive.

'But survive I did and a few weeks later I was taken back into the big ward with the other 30 or so patients ... I was eventually discharged from hospital after two-and-a-half years. The staff surse asked the Big White Chief for his prognosis, to which he replied he thought I could survive about 20 years, providing I looked after myself which would mean I would be in my middle forties.

'After a few months at home, my sister invited me to stay with her at Ancum in the Borders, as a sort of convalescence. Unfortunately, I took ill again after another few months and her GP suggested a return to hospital – a sanatorium at Hawick.

'I was awaiting availability of a bed there when, one night, this vision appeared at the foot of the bed. I recognised him as my grandfather and he said that I wasn't to worry as he was looking after me! I remember being very surprised that it was my grandfather as I had just been six when he died. My stay in the sanatorium lasted nearly two years again and then I was sent to Bangor Hospital in West Lothian for a thoracoplasty operation. When I finally arrived home, I was 28.

'I restarted work when I was 30 and retired at 65. I am now 78, have a wife who has taken great care of me, two grown-up children and four grandchildren!'

During Labour

Other experiences occurred during labour or childbirth. Twenty-three years ago, when Sharon Hawcutt was 18, her mother Doreen suddenly died from a heart-attack. Five months later, in January, Sharon was admitted to hospital as her baby was overdue. The next day she underwent an emergency Caesarean:

'While asleep, I had a dream (as I thought) of my mother. She was sitting beside me, dressed in a white lace dress and her head was covered with a white hood.

She began to talk to me but her lips weren't moving; we could read each other's thoughts. She told me I would have a baby girl, 7lb 1oz, and she would be OK after a while. She told me to tell my father that, when his time came, she would be waiting for him. She also said that I mustn't cry any more for her as she was always with me and then she was gone.

'Next thing, I came to in the recovery room. I told the nurse of my dream and what my mother had said but she told me that it was impossible to dream under anaesthetic because I was deeply unconscious. So I asked her, "What did I have?" "A girl." "How heavy?" "7lb 1oz." Was she OK? She was in the special baby care unit but would be fine. Two days later, she joined me on the ward.

'That same night, my mother appeared by my bed, and she spoke to me the same way through thought. She said I was going to be all right and that she loved me and to always remember she would always be with me – then she was gone.'

Before an Operation

One experience already described in Chapter 2 is Steve Cowling's encounter, in which he describes the dream he had before a major operation. In it, he boarded a steam train and at its destination he met with his father who gave him advice about a then unknown medical complication he had.

Pete Sangster recounts a similarly remarkable experience:

'In 1987, I suffered an industrial injury, prolapsing three discs in my lower back. I had worked for the local authority for some 17 years, driving dust wagons, salvage lorries, etc. This heavy work had taken its toll and my injury and subsequent enforced medical retirement were the result.

'Over the last 15 years, my condition has worsened,

becoming arthritic and affecting other joints in my body, particularly my knees. Earlier this year, I was referred for surgery and arthroscopy, recommended in the first instance to investigate what damage there was and the most appropriate treatment. I was uneasy about submitting for surgery but decided to go ahead, believing that things could only get better. My operation was duly arranged for August 2002.

'The day before I was due to go into hospital, I was at home, alone, preparing for my admission, packing a bag. Stopping for a cup of coffee, I sat on the front doorstep of our flat which opens on to an access corridor. I was not thinking of anything in particular but suddenly became aware that I was not alone. I looked up and, barely 3ft away, saw my mother standing there. She died in 1972 when I was 24 and looked no different to when I last saw her. I was stunned and could only stare. She reached out her hand and said, "Don't do it, son, don't do it." I looked away in disbelief and, when I looked back, she had gone.

'I was shaken and confused by what I had seen and telephoned my wife at work to tell her about it. Still feeling shaken, I went out on my bicycle to clear my head and to exercise the offending knee. While riding along the seafront promenade, I stopped for a breather and got chatting to an elderly gentleman whom I knew by sight. As we were talking, a man and his wife, whom I had never seen before, walked by. She was healthy but he was wearing wrap-around dark glasses, had a white stick and was leaning heavily on his wife's arm whilst dragging his left leg. As they passed, the gentleman I was talking to pointed him out to me. "Do you know what happened to him?" "No," I replied. "He went to hospital for a routine operation and had a stroke under the anaesthetic. Poor bugger's only 54!" I was shocked again, being 54 myself.

'After a few more minutes I continued my cycle ride, my mind still racing with the events of the morning and trying to rationalise what I had seen and heard. A little later, I stopped again on a different part of the seafront. This time I got into conversation with a chap who was a complete stranger to me. During the conversation, he pointed out some nearby flats and told me a story about a 54-year-old man who lived there and had suffered a stroke whilst under anaesthetic – the very same person I had been shown earlier!

'I was truly stunned by this time – first my mother and then being shown the same man, twice, by two different people, as an example of what could go wrong during surgery. I went straight home and cancelled my operation. I was prepared to live with the pain in my left knee for ever, rather than go against what appeared to be a clear warning ... but it doesn't end there.

'I went to bed that night as usual. When I woke up in the morning, I expected the usual struggle to get my knee moving. As it happened, I was able to stand up, straighten and flex my left knee without pain. I couldn't believe it and·tried bending and moving my leg in ways I'd not been able to for years. I expected it to be a fluke and revert to being painful but here we are – nearly three months on and still no pain. I can walk up the six flights of stairs to our flat without a twinge – unheard of before this.

'Make of this story what you will, but my wife and I firmly believe that my mother came to warn me against having the surgery and that I was shown the unfortunate man on the seafront as a demonstration of what would happen if I went under the anaesthetic. I have no explanation of this experience or my apparent healing and can only say, "Thank you, Mum."'

During Illness

Fifteen years ago, Mary Wilson was very ill with undiagnosed Lyme Disease:

'On one particular afternoon, I was alone in my living room, lying on the sofa. I had reached a stage in my illness where I'd begun to dread the passage of time, as it brought new symptoms and more pain. I was frightened that I might die before the doctors had found out what was wrong with me, and felt overwhelmed by loneliness.

'I noticed some kind of movement in front of a side window, and held my breath as an image of my mother (who had died seven years earlier) began to take form before me. Spellbound, I watched as she moved slowly around the room, turning on the spot every few seconds to become transformed into an image of herself at an earlier age. Her movements were extremely agile, in spite of having suffered with arthritis during the latter part of her life. It looked as if she was conducting some kind of fairy dance around me, her feet barely touching the ground. She never looked towards me, but I had the experience of being bathed in wave after wave of her concern, together with her reassurance that she was there to protect me.

'Then I sensed she was inviting me to go with her, there and then, to another place. I was suddenly filled with the fear of death and leaving my three young children. I spoke out to her, saying that I wasn't coming, that I would be all right, that I needed to stay behind. At that point, the image gently evaporated, absorbed into the light coming in through the side window.

'I felt guilty about having sent her away. But, shortly after that, my symptoms began to subside.

'Since then, I have often felt her presence. For example, when using her sewing machine, or baking the Christmas cake. Last month, my daughter arrived back home for her birthday. She rushed to join me in the kitchen, excitedly describing how, when she put her key in the lock, the door had swung open on its own and an extraordinary warm presence had welcomed and enfolded her. She said that she immediately knew it was her grandmother.'

Norma Parfitt was just three when her grandfather died:

'I knew he was still around but had just gone to live somewhere else. When I was five, I was very sick and was visited by people I knew to be past relatives, even though I did not know them – my grandfather was with them.'

This has been a chapter where the 'yes, but what if ...' of current marginal neuro-physiology begins to really challenge our understanding of apparently psychologically explicable phenomena. Psychologists would state that these accounts represent deep-seated recollections suppressed within our memory which surface under the influence of extreme stress and trauma when either spontaneously produced hormones in the brain or administered medication produce altered states of consciousness. Recent work by highly reputable and open-minded neuro-physiologists such as Dr Sam Parnia and Dr Peter Fenwick might suggest that, although it takes an altered mind to access this area, there are possibly entities being identified in quantum physics, between the spaces of DNA strands, which may represent much more of our life, spirit or soul than we currently understand and it may yet be discovered that the ability of these to move in both time and space may be responsible for our current mystification of the ability to communicate between what we call the living and the dead.

9

GLIMPSING THE OTHER SIDE

'The only true knowledge is knowing that you know nothing'
SOCRATES

SEEING A DECEASED LOVED one is almost mandatory in the realms of near-death and out-of-body experiences. As recipients enter the realm of light, accounts reveal how the person is met by the spirits of relatives and friends who have already passed over.

We know that there is no longer any question about the validity of near-death states. A few years back, people simply dismissed such accounts as nothing more than 'oxygen deprivation' or dream states, but recent research such as the Dutch Study[40] published in the *Lancet Medical Journal*[41] by cardiologist Pim van Lommel lays that to rest. So we know they happen and we know they exist.

The problem, however, is explaining *what* they are. We know now that the 'classical model' of an NDE takes the person out of their body and they float (as if a spirit) through a tunnel, encountering a bright and loving light, being met by deceased loved ones, knowing or being told, 'It isn't your time, you must return,' reviving back in the physical body. However, we must bear in mind that what people claim to see on 'The Other Side' of death is far more wide-ranging; descriptions given and how the episode is interpreted depend more on cultural traditions and language constraints than on what actually occurred.

The most common elements of an NDE based on P. Atwater's research base – which consisted of 3,000 adult and 277 child experiencers – were certainly out-of-body episodes, and an incredibly bright, loving light. Perhaps surprisingly, she reports that there aren't that many people who report 'tunnels'. Most people found themselves in another dimension fairly soon after they left their bodies and 'greeters' are commonplace – someone who suddenly appears and then acts as a guide. This is why this chapter is included in this book, for it is often only in an NDE or OBE that people meet with late relatives. As the majority of accounts show, these spirit greeters are deceased loved ones, or deceased pets. As in the chapter 'Angels of Death' in my last book, we know that visitations by angels, light beings and religious figures are also frequently reported.

The majority of experiences are positive, but it is important to note that, certainly, Atwater's research suggests the occurrence of unpleasant or hellish experiences to be one out of seven. Another researcher felt that one out of five was more accurate, and he may be right. These distressing near-death experiences are under-reported because people are either afraid or ashamed to admit they had one and, besides, it wouldn't make great bedtime reading! But happen they do.

After the experience is over, it isn't over. There are after-effects of physical changes (including unusual sensitivity to light and sound, electrical sensitivity, lower blood pressure, decreased tolerance of pharmaceuticals, to name but a few) and personality changes (latent abilities surface, some become more tolerant and emotionally expressive, smarter than before with perhaps enhanced creative or psychic abilities, others become more spiritual, and so forth). These experiences are transformative, and almost always have incredibly positive after-effects, taking away all fear of death and offering reassurance and the feeling that there is a reason they are still alive.

Major Explanations of the Phenomena

As modern medicine advances, people are being pulled back from death every day. However, it has been estimated that a staggering 40 per cent of them are claiming to have experienced another dimension of reality which, they claim, exists beyond death. Great debate surrounds this concept and is not something that I want to discuss here, as there is already an abundance of literature debating this issue.

From current research,[42] there is no one certain cause of the phenomenon although several plausible explanations have been put forward. First, their origins could be physiological or neurological. Research has shown that stimulation of certain areas of the brain's limbic system can cause an out-of-body sensation. It is also known that oxygen or sensory deprivation, or high fevers, can also cause the syndrome. Chemical activity in the brain (such as endorphins) may also provide a physiological explanation. Indeed, many do conclude that it is simply a condition that occurs when the brain is under stress or in the process of shutting down.

Another theory is that NDEs are pharmacological, meaning that certain drugs, depressants or anaesthetics have been known to cause an out-of-body sensation. The anaesthetic drug Ketamine has been claimed to give a perception of consciousness apart from the body, and could be responsible for seeing a light, feelings of love, etc. Nitrous oxide, which is used in some dental surgeries, is also frequently reported as causing the sensation. Illegal drugs such as marijuana and LSD are also causative. One study indicated that a staggering 44 per cent of marijuana users have had an out-of-body experience at some point.

On the other hand, it could be psychological. Intense fear has been known to cause an out-of-body-type sensation. For example, people have reported floating out of their bodies when a traffic accident seemed imminent, even though one never actually occurred. It has also been produced through hypnotic suggestion.

Such accounts could arguably have a paranormal or occultic origin. Contemporary occult groups and many ancient mystical religions report out-of-body experiences with similar characteristics to those of the NDE variety using various forms of meditation and techniques derived from such ancient occult manuals as *The Egyptian Book of the Dead* and *The Tibetan Book of the Dead*.

Whatever the stimuli, one thing is certain — such experiences are happening and are having a great effect on the person who experiences them.

Near-Death Experiences

The near-death phenomenon first came to real public attention back in 1977, when *Reader's Digest* published, in condensed form, the book *Life after Life* by psychiatrist Dr Raymond Moody. What this new-found knowledge and interest in NDEs has created is the revival of interest in the age-old questions about death and the possibility of an afterlife.

The reigning world view for much of the twentieth century in Western culture was that of Darwinian naturalism/materialism. Interestingly, this world view, which refuses to accept the possibility of the supernatural or the spiritual dimension, is now on the wane. Research into NDEs, as well as other brain research, is raising serious questions about the materialistic and monist[43] views of human nature.

Near-death experiences may occur during surgery, cardiac arrest, anaphylactic shock, coma, fever, anaesthetic, unconsciousness, accidents, physical injury, arrhythmia, seizures, suicide, severe allergic reactions and other physical trauma to the physical body. Near-death experiencers find themselves outside of their physical body. Their experience might include all or some of the following: going down a tunnel; seeing and/or entering a light; meeting a deceased relative or heavenly being; coming to a precipice or place where a decision about life or death must take place; seeing one's life pass before one's eyes, sometimes in order (called a 'life review'); acute awareness; a feeling of timelessness; and intense emotions.[44]

The sceptics arguments (and yes, there are many!) dismiss NDEs and put them down to some type of biological misfiring, but I am yet to find this plausible – the argument is most definitely lacking. There is not as yet any tangible, biological evidence of consciousness, memory, NDEs, etc. existing within the physical brain, and that this evidence can be collaborated by these sceptics. Secondly, they really need to prove how this biological consciousness can remain alive and capable of gathering information of the body's surroundings while the body is in a state of clinical death, showing no brain or heart or respiratory response of any kind, in order to promote their theory that humankind is wholly biological with no future beyond death.

Now, in the name of truth, the sceptics should present their biological proof (if it exists) or, until they do, cease and desist calling NDEs some sort of biological misfire. As it looks right now, I personally don't think such proof to be forthcoming.

So, ADCs and NDEs – from the letters I received, a handful talked about an ADC contained within an OBE or NDE. Had I wanted to study this section of ADCs alone, I would have specifically advertised or requested such information on the radio programmes where this was discussed, but I didn't. For a more in-depth look at this phenomenon, all one needs to do is look at some of the great books written which outline collected experiences – the vast majority contain an ADC of some sort. Below, however, are the ones that I received for this research.

Norma Lewis is a retired operating theatre nurse who, in 1996, developed painful allergic symptoms, with streaming eyes and burning skin. One evening, her symptoms flared up:

'As I was the only nurse on duty and there were two appendix operations to be done, I decided to stick it out to the end of my shift. By the time I was driving home, my eyes were so swollen I had one hand on the steering wheel and the other trying to keep my eyelids apart. My husband took me to casualty but it didn't help much and I came home.

'Then at about two in the afternoon, I collapsed in the bathroom. I was out of my body, looking down on myself. Then, to my amazement, I realised I was surrounded by 11 people, all the members of my close family who had passed away. There was my mother, just as she had always been, with her hair tied up in a scarf. There were also relatives there whom I had never met because they had died before I was born – but I somehow knew exactly who they were.

'All of them looked incredibly happy and serene. They were calling gently to me, "Come with us, come with us." I knew that, if I went with them, I would die, but that didn't frighten me.

'Then I found myself being shaken, and back in my body. I was being shaken awake by my panic-stricken husband. He was carrying me out of the bathroom. The next thing I knew two ambulance men were there. I was in hospital for five days and gradually made a complete recovery. There I was diagnosed as having a severe allergy over the years to the powder on the latex gloves we wear in the operating theatre. Sadly, I had to give up the job I loved. I've always been religious but now, after this experience, I know that death is nothing to fear.'

Another lady who had been diagnosed with a potentially fatal cancer and underwent major surgery wrote:

'Upon being wheeled back to my room, I experienced the most amazing vision. I was travelling through a "breathing" passage and found myself looking up into the most beautiful and magnificent domed area. It was gilded in bright, shining gold, and shone in the most amazing light. Smiling joyful "faces" I had known floated past me, all gazing at me as they passed, bathing me in their goodness ... Eventually, I was again travelling down the breathing passage towards a light. I never reached it, but gradually awoke. I felt I had been shown a part of heaven.'

Out-of-Body Experiences

The difference between NDEs and OBEs is that, although both involve out-of-body sensation, with an OBE the physical body is in absolutely no danger, and undergoes no form of trauma of any sort. Some people have reported OBEs which have occurred while jogging, performing on stage (especially in the case of musicians[45]), sleeping, praying, meditating, and some reports even describe OBEs while piloting fighter aircraft. Others report them while reading and while day-dreaming; however, they are most common during sleep.[46]

Dorothy Thomas's experience happened some 38 years ago:

'When I was 16 and sitting my O-levels, my father died at the young age of 53 years from cancer. At this time, 1964, cancer was relatively unheard of and we did not know what he was suffering from. He must have been in extreme pain and all we could do was sit and watch.

'When he passed away, we were all very, very sad and upset. It was the first time I had ever faced the death of a close loved one. My grandfather died when I was about nine or ten and, in those days, children were kept "aside", so as not to frighten us, I suppose. I also never knew my other grandparents as they had all passed long before I was born, so this was my real, first-hand experience of death.

'I had an exam on the morning after my father's

passing, and quite honestly I do not remember anything about it ... I had two or three more exams the following week and the funeral had to be planned around my timetable. Again, I remember nothing of those exams, but I passed them all with distinction. All my dear mother would say is, "Do your best, that's all Dad would ask of you." When I passed, she was so proud, as I'm sure my dad was also!

'It was three to four months after my dad passed that I had such a wonderful experience, that I have never had since ... I was still very depressed, crying a lot, not eating, not going to work and generally did not want to do anything except be with my dad. I was in bed and I saw a bright light and, as I looked up, I saw my dad. "I want to come up there with you, please!" He came towards me and reached down to take hold of my hand, but someone stepped towards me and said, "I'm sorry, love, but you must go back and look after your mum for me. When your time is right, I'll be waiting for you. I love you all and I'll be with you all." I cried and cried and cried because I felt "so near, so far".'

Alison Myers described a rather unusual OBE as a 'truly amazing, heart-stopping experience'. She writes:

'The dream occurred early this year, though I can't say exactly when. My mum had been dead nearly 17 years, my dad ten years and my brother just over two years. I hadn't dreamt about any of them for some time. In the dream, I found myself on a road that stretched off into the distance and Mum and Dad were suddenly with me, Mum on my left and Dad on my right. They were smiling at me and I was thrilled to find myself with them. I could sense the strength of their love for me and it filled me with a real joy. They asked me if I was ready to come with them. I said, "What do you mean, come with you?" and they explained that, if I wanted to, I could go with them, walk with them down the road towards the horizon and to whatever lay beyond. Now I couldn't see anything in the distance other than a glow of warm light over the horizon but when I looked in that direction I instantly knew that where the light was, my brother was, and that if I went with Mum and Dad I would also be reunited with him. I sensed his love for me emanating from the horizon and the fact that he was waiting for me, and I felt drawn to go and be with him and to stay in the company of my mum and dad. I felt rather shocked to be given such a momentous choice and, though my mind was trying to work out what this really meant, I got the general impression that if I went with them there would be no coming back. I remember being surprised that it could be so easy to cross over from this life to the next and it brought to mind Elijah being caught up in a chariot.

'Despite my shock and surprise, I was so happy to be with my parents and at the prospect of seeing my brother that, after a moment or two, I said, "Well, OK then, yes, why not? I wasn't expecting this but, yes, I'll come with you."

'My mum took hold of my left hand and smiled encouragingly at me, and my dad took my right hand and we began to walk down the road together. I was excited and had a strong sense that, when we got to where the light was over the horizon, I would know complete peace and happiness. But after we'd walked a little way, I suddenly stopped and said, "Hang on a minute, I can't do this!" and when they asked me "Why not?" I replied, "I can't leave Andrew!" The reality of my decision to go with them had finally registered. I was horrified at the thought of leaving my fiancé and partner of seven years on his own and was suddenly fully aware of the awful impact it would have on him and the grief he would feel. I said, "I can't leave him," and it was at about that point that I woke up.

'The dream was so real that when I woke I was seriously frightened. I was physically shaking, whimpering and my heart was pounding in my chest while my pulse was racing. I was very disoriented and it took several moments before I realised that I was in my bed with my fiancé beside me and that I was perfectly safe. I was astounded at the dream I'd just had, and the reason I was so frightened was because of how real it had been. I felt not that I'd been dreaming about something but that it had really happened, that I'd truly had the choice to go with Mum and Dad and, if I'd kept on going down that road, I would not have woken up. This dream was much more vivid than the other two and had an immediate physical effect as well as the longer-lasting emotional one. I have not had a dream like it before or since. It was a profound experience.'

Nancy Shapley writes:

'One evening, a few weeks after my mother had passed to the spiritual plane, she returned to prove that she is alive and well and pain free. This particular evening I felt a little tired so thought I would have a lie down on the divan. As soon as I did this, I found myself out of my body, standing in the hall of my home. I had the feeling that my mother was standing on the other side of the front door. I sent out a thought: "Walk through the door, Mum." She did, and we were hugging each other and all I could say was, "Oh Mum, Oh Mum." When I returned to my flesh body and opened my eyes, I realised we all have a solid spirit body.'

Another letter read:

'My mother found herself suddenly awake one night, floating above the bed and looking down on her own lifeless body. She could feel the presence of a woman in the corner of the room, a woman that she was sure she knew, but couldn't place. She felt great love and warmth from the woman and wanted to go higher so that she could be with her. The woman then spoke to her and said, "If you come any higher you will leave your body and never return. You have a choice, you can come with us now or you can stay here with your family, but staying will mean that you will have to suffer two years of pain and illness before you can join us again."

'My mother wanted so badly to go up towards the woman, such was the wondrous feeling of love and peace that was emanating from her. But, instead, she decided to take one last look at her sleeping children. She floated into each of their rooms and looked down on them as they slept, and then she returned to her own room and told the lady in the corner that she could not leave without saying goodbye. She chose the two years of pain.

'In the morning, she told my father what had happened and that same morning I was in my bedroom and felt a finger jabbing me in my side. I looked up and saw a lady dressed as a nun standing over me. I wasn't really concerned at the time, I just went into my parents' room and told my mummy that I had seen Florence Nightingale.

'Two months later, my mother was diagnosed with ovarian cancer. She suffered considerable pain and discomfort and eventually succumbed to the cancer. She died exactly two years to the day after her visitation.'

Marc Oxley's wife Amanda has convinced him that love does not die when our corporeal body does. He wrote:

'I loved her from the moment I saw her in 1984. It took five years for me to discover that she loved me, too. Within five months of making the discovery, in September 1989 we were married, despite her having been diagnosed with leukaemia in June of that year. She was 27, I was 35. We were deeply in love. I loved her so much it hurt (literally). But she never recovered from her illness and died on Boxing Day 1990.

'The spiritual link we had did not break. I was still in telepathic contact with her. This sounds mad but I was surrounded by her love. Many things happened ... her scent, items going missing, things moving and irresistible urges to do things which would prove to be pertinent of her – favourite records on the radio, sightings of dolphins in the Med, phone ringing both ends, etc.

'But the most amazing thing happened at Rheims on the way home from a holiday with her parents in March 1991. We stopped in a hotel on the way back to Calais and I had gone to bed after drinking half a bottle of wine. I was woken at 6.00am by a blackbird. There was a clock on the bedside table and it was starting to get light so I could read it easily. I had an overwhelming feeling that someone was in the room which frightened me, so I put my head under the covers, hoping it would go away. The bed then started to vibrate. The mattress felt like it was being thumped. I sat up in response and saw at the bottom of the bed what I can only describe as a large diamond, rotating slowly. This puzzled me, understandably, and, as I watched, Amanda's face appeared in the centre. I shouted out her name, I was exhilarated to see her. Then she was with me in the room, kneeling on all fours on the bed, wearing a white gown, her face was radiant. She was as pleased to see me as I was her.

'She moved up the bed and then lay down in my arms. I cannot tell you how happy I was to see her. I stroked her face and kissed her. She was as solid as the last time I had held her. I told her how much I missed her and she spoke to me saying she loved me, too. It was amazing ... we chatted for some time and I find it hard to understand this bit, but we went to the Tivoli Gardens in Rome. We strolled around hand in hand, so happy to be reunited. On our return to the room in Rheims, I pinched myself, as I was sure I was dreaming. It hurt ... she was still there. I looked around and saw the room in detail – the cigarettes in the ashtray, the bottle of wine, my clothes in a heap. I looked back and there she was! I thought, I am dreaming and as such I will turn you into a two-headed monster. She smiled and went to bite my hand, which was busy stroking her face (this was one of her favourite tricks when she was alive). She then slowly faded away. Smiling all the while, I was beside myself with joy. I looked at the clock and saw it was 6.45am.

'I wanted to go and tell her parents but thought it was too early. I needed time to think, to digest what had happened. I got off the bed, had a cigarette and stood staring out the window until I felt composed enough to go and see them. I did not go back to sleep after she left, I was awake the whole time. She is still with me but not as close as she was that morning.'

A similar type of experience afflicted Carl Jung, the renowned psychiatrist who founded his own school of psychology. He relates a meditative ADC in his book *Memories, Dreams, Reflections* whereby, while awake in bed one night, Carl feels the presence and has 'an inner visual image' of a friend who died recently. At the man's insistence, Carl follows him (in his mind) to the man's home and into his library. His friend shows him the second of five books with red covers that are on a high shelf, and the ADC ends.

Filled with curiosity, Carl visits his friend's library the next day. He stands on a stool to examine the five red volumes and finds they are novels written by Emile Zola. The second one is titled *The Legacy Of The Dead*.

For whatever reason it seems there is so much in the way, be it as much as a suppression of knowledge or whatever, that the general consensus for some time has been to tell the general public or experiencers that NDEs and OBEs are merely biological events. What gets me is that, as human beings, we do have a right to know about this and not have things explained away for the sake of it – especially if they are real occurrences and can help us understand ourselves and learn to grow spiritually.

So, the big question – can NDEs and OBEs help us to ascertain whether we do, in fact, survive death? Is there an afterlife? Indeed for several years I have grappled with this very question and do think that as spontaneous, non-induced experiences go (in other words not including mediums and psychics as part of this argument), then yes, such experiences are as conclusive as proof gets. The arguments and scientific findings regarding consciousness, with which OBEs and NDEs provide us, seem to direct us to clear, solid proof that we as humans are indeed spiritual 'beings' simply inhabiting a physical body. And that the evidence is already here, but our scientific knowledge is not yet sufficient to reproduce it or demonstrate it.

I shall end here by saying that this failure of science to be able to explain these phenomena is well demonstrated and I think summed up by the following extract[47] where physical events were not fully explicable by the science of that time:

'Alexander Graham Bell, inventor of the telephone, was urged by his family to seek psychiatric evaluation. His insistence the human voice could be sent great distances through a wire caused them concern over his mental health.

'If Bell's family had seen a modern television receiver in operation they would have really been surprised. This form of transmitting and receiving data without wires was yet to be discovered.

'Alexander Graham Bell and his family would have believed the television receiver was the source of the images and sounds it presented. That the images/sounds were stored somewhere within, and different groups shown when the position of the "channel knob" was adjusted. Bell might even have removed the cover to look for them, trying to discover how the thing worked. But, no matter how hard or long he examined the television receiver, he would not have found the images and sounds it presented stored within.

'Science has a similar problem with the human brain. Your body is a "tool of communication" for your consciousness (the real you) to use while exploring the physical realm. No matter how hard or long scientists look in the brain for things like consciousness, memory, mind, personality, dreams, NDEs, OBEs, etc. they will not be found. The brain is not the source of these events. There is no proof that the Near Death Experience, or any other event for that matter, originates within the brain. Nothing has been found stored there. Stimulating the brain at different points to produce different events doesn't prove any of those events are stored within the brain. Just as adjusting (stimulating) the "channel knob" on a TV doesn't prove the images/sounds produced are stored within the TV.'

10

PETS RETURN

'The comfort of having a friend may be taken away,
but not that of having had one'

SENECA

PET DEATH IS SOMETHING WHICH, over the last few years, has sprung up more and more in the media as part of a wider acceptance of death and bereavement in today's society. There are several pet cemeteries and pet crematoria in Britain which have hit the headlines with their newsworthy combination of meeting a real need and sentimentalising of animal death.[48] The Cambridge Pet Crematorium and Cemetery (see Resources at the back of this book), for example, featured as a major story in the *Radio Times*.[49]

Back in 1992, Professor Douglas Davies carried out a UK survey in which he explored pet death,[50] and in answer to the question, 'Do you think animals have souls?' 77 per cent said yes they did, 6 per cent said no, while 15 per cent said they didn't know.

We all know people who are incredibly attached to their pets, and that some human–animal relationships are, in fact, profound, leaving the left owners just as bereaved as when a member of their family dies. Some more so. It has been pointed out to me that a pet is there 24/7 by your side; to suddenly have it taken away from you can often leave more of a void and sense of loss than a relative ever could.

Interestingly, an earlier survey of Davies's[51] revealed that 55 per cent of dog owners and 44 per cent of cat owners celebrated their pets' birthdays; that 77 per cent of respondents' cats slept on their owners' beds, as did 48 per cent of respondents' dogs. Approximately 80 per cent of these pet owners were aware of the anniversary of their pets' death. Practically all talked to their pets and also reckoned that their pets were members of the family. It is possible to analyse this strength of feeling that some owners have for their pets by asking them what sort of status they believe their pet has a place in the family unit. The results were as follows:

> Equal adult members of the family:
> 19% (dogs)   23% (cats)
> junior members of the family:
> 25% (dogs)   25% (cats)
> animal members of the family:
> 54% (dogs)   51% (cats)

By amalgamating all of this together, it is not so hard for non-pet owners to grasp the sense of grief the pet's death brings and the fact that animal afterlife is seen as a natural progression to the beliefs surrounding a human afterlife.

Barbara Gilbert's letter was the first I opened. It began: 'My story is not about a human, but my beloved dog who died nine years ago last September ...' Without thinking, I put it to one side. However, slowly the pile became higher as more letters outlined accounts with deceased pets. Having not specifically asked for accounts of people seeing pets return, the ones recorded below slipped though the net. I imagine if I had specifically asked for such experiences, the results would have been tenfold.

Barbara's letter continues:

'I came home from work on New Year's Eve about three months after my dog had passed. I was looking out of my kitchen window and I saw my beloved Reuben (he was a red boxer) in the garden. I could not believe my eyes.'

In her book *Pathway To The Spirit World* Hashi-Hanta discusses her poodle, Chum Boy, dying when she was away from home. However, he returned to visit her to say goodbye twice. Wide awake she sees him run into her bedroom, jump up on to her bed and into her arms. She holds him briefly both times and notices he is younger and fully restored to health.

Hilary Price also mentioned in passing how she has awoken on several occasions to feel and see her late cat Misty curled up on top of her feet at the bottom of her bed. Each time she has reached out to stroke her she has 'melted' away. Such an experience is so common. Many people have mentioned seeing deceased animals, albeit briefly, perhaps curled up at the foot of their bed, or in a favourite place on the sofa, or, like Barbara, playing in the garden. Others hear their pets, as did Judy with her eight-month old pet cat, Magic, who had disappeared.

'About seven to ten days after her disappearance, I awoke to her meowing loudly in my right ear, as she often did when she was hungry and wanted me to get up and feed her. At first, I thought I had been dreaming when I woke up, but I continued to hear the meowing from the living room, which is just off our bedroom. I jumped out of bed screaming, "Magic! Magic!" but I couldn't find her anywhere. I must have spent a good hour looking behind furniture, in other rooms, under the bed, and calling her continuously. I was completely baffled but, later, I decided that I must be grieving much more than I had been willing to admit. However, her visits continued ... the last one being about five days ago.'

As with relatives, a familiar smell has been reported on several occasions. Both Richard Giles and his friend Andy Weekes smelled the familiar smell of Richard's family dog a good six months after he had passed.

'For 13 years, we had a daft basset-hound dog who was the heart of the family and adored by us all. During the last three years of his life, he suffered liver problems and arthritis, finally taking a turn for the worse and dying in December 2001.

'In the mid-summer of 2002, a friend and I had a strange experience when we arrived home at around 2.00am. As we entered through the front door, the entire hallway was filled with the warm fuzzy smell of Droopy. My friend Andy and I turned to each other and simultaneously said, "Oh my God ... it smells like Droopy." People may assume that it could have been a simple build up of smells in the carpets and in the furniture, but why would this smell suddenly occur without reason at 2.00am on a summer's night, and then immediately disappear? It's not logical! Also, the theory of another dog being in house at the time isn't credible as we have never replaced Droops. The only conclusion we can draw is that this was a communication from Droopy that we, as humans, are yet to understand.'

Now, while many people are greeted by a 'Being of Light' or a deceased love one, some people report having been greeted by beloved deceased animals, as did Jackie Jones-Hunt whose NDE involved travelling on a train and, if she had boarded it, she knew she would not be coming back:

'I haemorrhaged and that is when my late grandfather and beloved dog came to assist me, and that which my granddad said was verified by the doctors! [He had told me I had] a blood clot on a lung and that I needed to sit if I could to save my life. During the night in hospital, my dog was lying against my right calf, where they found the beginning of a deep vein thrombosis due to the haemorrhage.'

Garth wrote of his experiences with his cats:

'My wife and I had recently had to give permission to our vet to put down our beloved Burmese tom cat, Sam. He was 12 years old, had been suffering from what had originally been diagnosed as chronic kidney deterioration but, during his last couple of days of life, the vet had carried out a biopsy and discovered that Sam had cancer on one of his kidneys. This devastated us because Sam had been a very special animal and we couldn't contemplate the idea of losing communication with him. To understand this it is necessary for me to digress a little regarding his character and our relationship, which is not so very commonplace between most cat owners and their pets, but tends to be fairly characteristic of owners of Burmese cats, who seem to have something particularly spiritual in their natures, especially their capacity for love.

'I have always believed that part of the responsibility of being a pet owner is to contribute to their evolution by "educating" them about as much as possible regarding their environment and life in general. Consequently, from the time Sam was a baby kitten, I had taken him for walks, taken him out in the car, shown him people swimming and boating in the sea (the expression in his eyes was something to see!), taken him to the railway station to see trains with people getting on and off them, played him classical music and showed him pictures in books (he was particularly fascinated by brightly coloured pictures of ancient Egypt and the pyramids!).

'I work at home, essentially alone, although Sam

would sit in the chair opposite me while I typed away on the computer, and then at the same time every day, when he considered I had been working long enough, he would come over on to my chest and try to get me to stop typing, or else he would just watch the cursor moving over the screen and then work out the connection between the key-strokes and the appearance of letters, and watch bemusedly as pictures would change on the screen and all kinds of inexplicable phenomena that were part of my electronic human experience presented themselves to him. Like most cats, he had adjusted to television and the telephone long ago and took them in his stride.

'Obviously, our relationship had become very, very special over the years. My wife and I were heartbroken as we held him while he was put down. My problem was not so much accepting that we had had to put him out of pain; that was obvious. It was the sense of complete finality, and the feeling that all of that communication I had spent so many years building between us and all that evolutionary progress Sam had made was suddenly for nothing, gone, obliterated, all for nothing. I couldn't accept easily the inference that there was nothing left of him, that he was just a body. That lively intelligence, the look of love in his eyes and his insistence on expressing every cat opinion in loud stentorian tones and his social graces and cat etiquette, all extinguished in a moment.

'My wife and I both found it very difficult to cope with for many weeks, even though she was convinced that animals had souls which survived death. She believed that Burmese cats' souls would join a kind of group Burmese soul, but I hated the thought that Sam would lose his individuality and become just part of an amorphous mass soul.

'Ten years earlier, we had lost another cat, Tara, who

also died of kidney failure. She had been alive when we obtained Sam and upon her death it seemed as though Sam had somehow immediately assimilated many of her personality traits, including the way he played games from that day on, his understanding of the vocabulary we used to talk to him, which had seemed to evoke no response prior to Tara's death, but which he seemed to understand immediately once she had died. So I had thought that my wife was probably right and that there was a universal Burmese soul into which Sam had been assimilated and that was that.

'But we continued to grieve for him and would send him little messages mentally, in case he were "around" somewhere.

'Then I had this experience. I was barely awake, but what had awakened me slightly was the feeling that I was lying on top of a cat, with my arms holding him very close to my chest. I could feel him purring and hear him purring. The vibration of the purrs was resonating in my chest and his purrs were continuous and fairly high-pitched, of a kind he always gave when he was deliriously happy. I didn't know how I could be lying on top of him, although I do tend to, and was lying on my stomach, but that made it seem impossible anyway. But there he was. At least, I assumed it was Sam.

'But as soon as it became apparent to me that I was hugging this cat tightly to me, and it was an unmistakable sensation, one that I couldn't deny or put down to illusion, I immediately began to question the identity of the cat. Was it Tara or Sam? I kept trying to answer that question but the more intently I asked the question and tried to work out which cat it was, the fainter grew the purrs and I felt him or her diminishing and fading away. The experience lasted for about 20 seconds, I would estimate.

'I was awake then and woke my wife and told her.
There is no question in my mind that it was not a dream.
It was too physically real and even today I can recall the
sensation of the purring vibrating against my chest.
Since that day, as a consequence of this "visit", I have
been reading books on life after life and it has
completely reoriented my consciousness towards
accepting survival. Perhaps Sam thought it was time my
evolution was furthered and that was one way he knew
of ensuring it. I now believe that we shall meet again one
day and that has given both my wife and me great hope
and inspiration.'[52]

Now, as with relatives and friends who appear with some sort of
ADC pre-empting their death, encounters are the same with pets,
as Sara Dann explains:

'I have a lovely story of my recently deceased cat Holly
who made contact with me. While on holiday in Italy, I
had a "dream" about her – she was somehow at a
crossroads, a place very green and with two paths to go
down. I can only describe this place as a green square
with leafy avenues leading off it, like a London park.

'A faceless stranger was trying to get her down one
path and she resisted, looking at me, and saying it's OK,
I know which way to go. I reassured her and off she went
down the other path – she kept looking back at me and
I kept telling her that it was OK.

'On waking up, I told my husband about this pleasant
dream I had of Holly ... neither of us thought any more
of it.

'However, less than two hours later, a phone call from
the cattery told us that Holly had died peacefully in her
sleep. At first, I was very, very upset, but Phil later said
maybe it was Holly letting me know that she was going

and that she went peacefully. This gave me great comfort; also, it shows how much she loved me. We talked and had a great understanding – which some people think stupid. However, I know differently.'

And finally, we will end with one of my favourite ADC experiences, featuring Thor. Marilyn Evans is well known as an animal healer in the West Country. At the time, she ran a small wild bird and animal hospital where Thor, a beautiful white swan, was taken in, badly oiled, with an injured leg, and had lost his beloved mate:

'It took just an hour to make contact with him and gain his confidence and he allowed me to stroke him. His response was to put his neck around mine and totally relax. We were friends! After that, I cleaned him in our bath. Thor wandered around the garden during the day; at night, I tucked him under my arm, carried him upstairs and he bedded down in the bathroom, quietly "talking" and honking to me.

'After nine months, Thor decided it was time to return to the wild ... he was released on the Tamar at Moditonham Quay, near Saltash, where he was first rescued and brought to us. Through the *Sunday Independent* and various contacts I found, he had "emigrated" over to Torpoint in Cornwall.

'One Christmas Eve at 10.00pm, we had an urgent police message – a swan was in trouble at Torpoint. My husband Dennis and I immediately drove over there but all the swans seemed all right. Three days later, another urgent message came and this time I found Thor lying on the beach – he was in a terrible state, unable to hold his head up fully and breathing with great difficulty. He'd been washed in and out by the tide for days ...

'Gathering him in my arms, I placed his soft neck

around mine and we all drove home in quietness. I knew the earthly end was near for him. The following evening, at 10 o'clock, Thor quietly and peacefully died in my arms ...

'One evening, four years later, I was stunned to find Dennis had quite suddenly left his earthly body, too, sitting in his chair just minutes after we had been talking about animal healing.

'At his semi-military funeral, the weather was grey and drizzling. After the service, we came to the graveside unable to see more than a few yards through the gloom.

'A bugler sounded "The Last Post" and, as the last, deeply moving notes died away in the still air, a shaft of light lit up the scene. I felt a sudden sense of awe. Three mourners asked me if I had seen the extraordinary beam of light. Each described "a swan with outstretched wings". That is why a swan is carved on Dennis's headstone.'

To conclude, there is little doubt that such experiences closely resemble the experiences of the human dead. As Douglas Davies writes, 'The way in which the death of pets fits into the overall scheme of human bereavement should not be ignored, for it affords a window into the significance of relationships for particular individuals ... attitudes to the death of pets is also one way of reflecting on wider attitudes to human life and death.'[53]

POSTSCRIPT

'When the earth shall claim your limbs,
then shall you truly dance'

KAHIL GIBRAN

AS CAN BEEN SEEN throughout the previous chapters, these after-death communications can clearly happen at any time – be it preceding the death, or moments, days, months or even years after. It is clear that the majority of them happen at a time when the recipient is actually undergoing the grieving process with the experience acting for many as a huge milestone ... from it, they are often able finally to accept the loss and move forward.

As from the outset, the important emphasis to attach to these ADC experiences is the fact that, for the vast majority, the living person was not actively seeking to establish contact with the deceased – the experiences listed here were almost exclusively spontaneous occurrences; they were not invoked or relayed via a medium or psychic.

The question remains – who is it who reached out to the bereaved? Is it the spirit of the deceased, the unconscious, God or some supreme force? If you are expecting an answer, I am afraid I cannot offer it.

So what are we to make from these experiences – what can we take from them?

How Can the ADCs be Utilised?

We can ascertain that this phenomenon is widespread. Internationally, there are no barriers as to who can and is reporting them. So why has it consistently been overlooked by those who have not had the experience and are unable to grasp its impact?

One thing I found both intriguing and maddening after the publication of *Seeing Angels* was how many friends, colleagues and relatives came up to me and said, 'Actually, I didn't want to say anything to you before, but I have actually had an experience like that ...' Again, fear of ridicule or being alone or being seen as slightly nuts were all reasons for the silence. However, after reading the book, they felt slightly relieved at how common their encounter was.

Depending on the belief systems of the bereaved and the type of experience which takes place, the spontaneous occurrence of an ADC can be used in many ways. Here is a partial list of possibilities drawn up by certified grief counsellor Dr Louis LaGrande, at the State University of New York. He believes the bereaved can develop from them with the help of a support person (a family member, close friend or counsellor). The suggested benefits of ADCs are:

- To express emotions which one has difficulty putting into words. Expressing emotions is an essential factor in dealing with any major loss experience.

- To help establish a new relationship with the deceased loved one. Establishing a new relationship with the deceased, one which features positive memories and acceptance of his/her absence, is one of the normal factors which causes active grief to take a lengthy period to reconcile.

- To accept the death of the loved one, which is a primary task of grieving. Acceptance on an intellectual level is quite different from accepting the death of a loved one on an emotional level. This is one reason why the grief process takes so much longer than the general public realises.

- To create rituals to say goodbye, to reconcile differences or to establish a sense of continuity. Rituals are critical grieving tools which can bring structure and a sense of direction and control when life seems to be out of control.

- To stimulate the creation of positive memories of the deceased loved one. Loving memories of our deceased loved ones are important sources of consolation and stress reduction.

- To re-establish hope. Hope, consciously or unconsciously fostered, is life-affirming. The extraordinary experience can be a major source for rekindling hope.

- To eliminate unnecessary suffering from excessive guilt, anger or depression.

- To help establish a new identity. [54]

Final Thoughts

I have asked colleagues and close friends to read through parts of this manuscript as I went along and during the whole writing process several questions have been raised. What is the point of regurgitating a book mainly full of ADCs, and what can be gained from them?

Should I have a Conclusion, or at least a 'tentative' Conclusion, as I called it in the last book? Indeed, is there a Conclusion? I have decided not – hence the header to this closing section.

Indeed, I myself have no answers to these questions, but I am further along the path of understanding these experiences than I was when I first began – I hope you have gained from these pages as well.

Conclusions are things people expect and perhaps even want or need. We want scientific certainties, 'yes' or 'no'. We yearn for rationality and logic, needing to be able to stand back and see the scientific processes or line of thought. But I do not want this to be a pseudo-scientific book. It is what it is ... take from it and make from it what you can and will.

Pseudo-scientists aspire to these standards – they want their work to be taken seriously but I am content to accept these ADCs as being important to recipients' lives. I don't want or need to draw judgements on them – for one, I do not feel it appropriate or useful. I am relaying people's stories which I think speak for themselves.

I think, for many, accepting the reality of an after-death communication is a big leap of faith – as is the notion for our culture of survival after death. Having said this, though, if you talk to people about the idea, you will likely find many acquaintances who have had something of this inexplicable nature happen to them – as I have found while writing this book.

As mentioned before, however, it is not sufficient to say that the situation of stress or distress is an adequate explanation without consideration of the possibility of the existence of some as yet immeasurable but nonetheless evident entity in ourselves which appears to have the possibility of transcending our current time and space (in other words, living on and surviving death on a different plane). The speed at which research in this area is able to move forward is largely dependent upon man's open-mindedness to more spiritual things and his search to produce rational explanation. If one believes that our life 'Force' or creative force or God, however one wants to describe it, would wish us to use our brains to understand and appreciate the magnificence of our world and existence, then one must also believe that sooner or later man will become closer in our understanding of our spiritual links with this Force. Some people would say that we are attempting to equate with or supersede this force, whereas in fact greater understanding of it would almost certainly produce greater awe of it and a closer relationship with it. The fact that science can dissect a tree and follow its journey from seed through germination to maturity does not take away the fact that the tree exists, is miraculous and we are still unable to make one ourselves. The fact we understand it through and through does not lessen the reality and enormity of it. The same goes with the spirit world. To understand and accept it is there, and to learn to appreciate how we interact with it, in no way lessens the wonder of it.

Whatever the conclusions and realities really are, there is one thing which I really do know is certain, and it is this – to the people who are fortunate enough to experience an ADC, all are totally convinced that they have been in touch with another reality or dimension, one that is equally as real and meaningful as the physical reality they live and grieve in each day.

For more information and to submit accounts ...

As this book comes full circle, I will leave you in the hands of the very people from whom this book took its inspiration. Firstly, The ADC Project is fast becoming international and online is a vast forum for sharing information and research on After-Death Communication and related spiritual subjects. I hope this book has not only sparked interest this side of the pond but will also help expand Bill and Judy's important and much-needed research even more. Secondly, I would like to also point you in the direction of the ADCRF. I suggest, if sending accounts, you submit to both and certainly if you are seeking more information or want to research this field more thoroughly then these are certainly the two main organisations you need to begin with.

The Guggenheims' ADC Project
If you would like to learn more about the Guggenheims' ADC Project, the internet site is http://www.after-death.com. To submit

an ADC of your own to add to the vast database, you can do so by email or snail mail:

    Email: adc-project@After-death.com

    Address: The ADC Project, PO Box 916070, Longwood, Florida 32791, United States of America

The After-Death Communication Research Foundation

The After-Death Communication Research Foundation (ADCRF, www.adcrf.org) was established in 1999 to encourage submission of ADC accounts, and to share these accounts with the world. This website was founded by Jeffrey Long, M.D., a physician practising the speciality of radiation oncology (the use of radiation to treat cancer). Jody Long is the ADCRF webmaster and a practising attorney. At the current time, over 400 ADC accounts have been shared and over 200 experiences posted on the ADCRF website. The ADCRF website contains a very detailed questionnaire regarding the ADC experience. This questionnaire allows a unique opportunity to research aspects of the ADC experience not previously investigated. It is expected that new insights regarding ADC will result from this process. Jeff and Jody Long are already very clear from the experiences shared that ADC is a real experience of significance and meaning. Often the ADC experience can be positively life-changing.

Jeff and Jody recognise that ADC is only one important part of a spectrum of meaningful spiritual experiences. Their other websites devoted to experiences related to ADC include: Near-Death Experience Research Foundation (www.nderf.org) and Out-of-Body Experience Research Foundation (www.oberf.org, devoted to out-of-body experiences and other spiritually transformative experiences). Like the Guggenheims' site, Jeff and Jody's sites have nothing for sale, and they do not solicit contributions. They believe it is an important part of their life to share freely with the world the inspiring accounts that have been shared freely with them on their websites.

BEREAVEMENT GROUPS AND ORGANISATIONS

A B Welfare and Wildlife Trust
7 Knox Road
Harrogate
North Yorkshire
HG1 3EF
Tel: 01423 530900/868121
The only charity in the country able to advise dying and
bereaved people on any type of funeral in any type of place,
anywhere in the country. In constant need of funds to continue
to provide the free advice service and train volunteers.

Age Concern
207 Pentonville Road
London
N1
Tel: 020 7278 1114
http://www.helptheaged.org.uk
Fact sheets and information on all aspects of death and
bereavement, also offers a will-writing service.

Alzheimer's Disease Society
Gordon House
10 Greencoat Place
London
SW1P 1PH
Tel: 020 7306 0606
Email: info@alzheimers.org.uk
http://www.alzheimers.org.uk
Advice and information on support and services.

Another Way
c/o South West Environmental Action Project
17 Castle Street
Kirkcudbright
DG6 4JA
Scotland
Tel: 01557 331993
Email: sweapk@cqm.co.uk
Voluntary organisation offering information, advice and support
for death and bereavement.

Asian Family Counselling Service
76 Church Road
Hanwell
London
W7 8LB
Tel: 020 8567 5616
Email: afcs99@hotmail.com

Association of Burial Authorities
155 Upper Ground
London
N1 1RA
Tel: 020 8288 2522
Fax: 020 8288 2533
http://www.aba@swa-pr.com.uk

Association for Children with Life-threatening Terminal Conditions and Their Families (ACT)
Orchard House
Orchard Lane
Bristol
BS1 5DT
Tel: 0117 922 1556
Fax: 0117 930 4707
Email: info@act.org.uk
http://www.act.org.uk
Offers advice and information.

The Befriending Network
Claremont
24–27 White Lion Street
London
N1 9PD
Tel: 07041 420 192 (London and national enquiries)
Email: info@befriending.net
http://www.befriending.net
Befriending network of trained volunteers active in North and West London, but can provide referrals to other agencies in other areas. Support for terminal and life-threatening illnesses.

Bereavement UK
http://www.bereavementuk.co.uk

British Association for Counselling
1 Regent Place
Rugby
Warwickshire
CV21 2PJ
Tel: 01788 578328/9
http://www.counselling.co.uk
Will provide details of counselling organisations and services in your local area.

Bereavement Register

To register details, contact: 0870 600 7222
Aims to supply names of the recently deceased to mail order
companies to ensure that names and addresses are removed from
their databases so that mailings are not sent out, causing distress
to the bereaved and embarrassment to the companies.

British Holistic Medical Association

59 Landsdowne Place
Hove
East Sussex
BN3 1FL
Tel/Fax: 01273 725951
Self-help tapes and relaxation techniques.

British Humanist Association

47 Theobald's Road
London
WC1X 8SP
Tel: 020 7430 0908
http://www.humanism.org.uk/funerals.asp
Information on non-religious funerals, including suggested
readings and pieces of music. Can also provide an officiant.

British Medical Association

BMA House
Tavistock Square
London
WC1H 9JP
Tel: 020 7387 4499
Fax: 020 7383 6400
http://www.bma.org.uk
Governing body for the British medical profession.

The Buddhist Hospice Trust

c/o Dennis Sibley
1 Laurel House
Trafalgar Road
Newport
Isle of Wight
PO30 1QN
Tel: 01983 526945
Email: dsibley@ukonline.co.uk
http://www.buddisthospice.cjb.net
Established in 1986 to explore Buddhist approaches to dying,
death and bereavement. It is non-sectarian and welcomes both
Buddhists and non-Buddhists alike. Offers emotional support and
spiritual help for the dying and bereaved. Buddhist volunteers
will visit dying and bereaved people.

Call Centre (Cancer Aid and Listening Line)

Swan Buildings
20 Swan Street
Manchester
M4 5JW
Tel: 0161 835 2586 (National helpline, manned
Monday–Thursday, 12 noon–3pm and 7.30–10.30pm,
emergencies dealt with at any time)
Practical advice and emotional support for cancer patients and
families.

The Cambridge Pet Crematorium

Howard Jonas – General Manager
Thriplow Heath
Nr Royston
Hertfordshire
SG8 7RR
Tel: 01763 208295
Email: mail@cpc-net.co.uk

http://www.cpc-net.co.uk
CPC has over 20 years' experience in pet cremation and
bereavement care and provides a range of cremation services to
bereaved pet owners throughout England from individual to
communal cremation. Equal respect is given to all companion
animals, performing cremations with care and dignity.

Cancer BACUP
3 Bath Place
Rivington Street
London
EC2A 3JR
Tel: 020 7696 9003
Fax: 020 7696 9002

Cancer Information Helpline Service
0808 800 1234
(Staffed by specialist nurses Monday–Friday 9am–7pm)
http://www.cancerbacup.org.uk
Cancer BACUP provides information and support to people
affected by cancer.

Cancerlink
11–21 Northdown Street
London
N1 9BN
Freephone cancerlink 0808 808 0000
Email: cancerlink@cancerlink.org.uk
Referral service with details of local self-help groups and
some helpful pamphlets.

Cancer Relief Macmillan Fund

15–19 Britten Street
London
SW3 3TZ
Tel: 020 7351 7811
Fax: 020 7376 8098
http://www.macmillan.org.uk

The fund provides financial assistance for some cancer patients
and helps fund organisations caring for cancer patients.
Macmillan nurses can help with emotional support, pain and
symptom control.

Chai-Lifeline, Jewish Cancer Support and Health Centre

Norwood House
Harmoney Way
off Victoria Road
Hendon
London
NW4 2BZ
Tel: 020 8202 4567

Works with young people and adults facing life-threatening
illnesses by providing support groups and complementary
therapies.

The Child Bereavement Trust

Aston House
West Wycombe
High Wycombe
Buckinghamshire
HP14 3AG
Tel: 01494 446648
Fax: 01494 440057
Email: enquiries@childbereavement.org.uk
http://www.childbereavement.org.uk

The Child Bereavement Trust provides support and counselling for grieving families. It is a charity that cares for bereaved families by training and supporting professional carers. Established in 1994 by Jenni Thomas and Julia Samuel, it aims to increase awareness and acknowledge the importance of grief and loss.

It offers a number of helpful books and videos for grieving families as well as professionals. There is also an Information and Support Line for professionals caring for bereaved families. It is available on 0845 357 1000 between 9am and 5pm.

Great Ormond Street also offers a Child Death Helpline on 020 7813 8160.

Compassionate Friends
53 North Street
Bristol
BS3 1EN
Tel: 0117 953 9639
Email: info@tcf.org.uk
http://www.tcf.org.uk
A self-help group for parents who have lost a son or daughter of any age.

Cruse Bereavement Care
Cruse House
126 Sheen Road
Richmond
Surrey
TW9 1UR
Tel: 020 8940 4818
Fax: 020 8940 7638
Bereavement Helpline: 020 8332 7227
To speak to a counsellor, afternoons or evenings, phone 0345 585 565
Email: info@crusebereavementcare.org.uk
http://www.crusebereavementcare.org.uk

Cruse Bereavement Care exists to promote the wellbeing of bereaved people and to enable anyone suffering a bereavement caused by death to understand their grief and cope with their loss.

Cruse is now the largest bereavement counselling charity in the world and has nearly 200 branches throughout the UK and will provide a contact number for a local branch. It offers confidential counselling and support and can also offer advice on practical matters. The mail– order service offers more than 100 books, booklets and pamphlets designed to help the bereaved and those that support them.

Disaster Action

17 Bruno Court
10 Fassett Square
London
E8 1BF
Tel: 020 7254 7111
Press Office Tel/Fax: 01483 799 066
http://www.disasteraction.org.uk
Self-help group for those bereaved by a major disaster such as a plane crash.

The Foundation for the Study of Infant Deaths (FSID)

Artillery House
11–19 Artillery Row
London
SW1P 1RT
Enquiries: 020 7222 8001
24-hour helpline: 020 7233 2090
Fax: 020 7222 8002
24-hour helpline: 020 7235 1721
Email: fsid@sids.org.uk
http://www.sids.org.uk
The UK's leading cot-death charity working to prevent sudden and unexpected infant deaths and promote baby health. FSID

works towards these aims by funding research, supporting bereaved families and promoting advice on how to reduce the risk of cot-death to parents and professionals.

Gilda's Club

14 Bury Place
London
WC1A 2JL
Tel: 020 7440 9150
http://www.gildas.org
Founded in New York in 1995 by actor Gene Wilder in memory of, and inspired by, his wife, comedienne Gilda Radner, there is now a Gilda's Club London. It acts as a free resource for men, women, children and teenagers with cancer and their families, with support, workshops, networking groups and social events.

Healthy Gay Living Centre

40 Borough High Street
London
SE1 1XW
Tel: 020 7407 3550
Fax: 020 7407 3551
Now encompasses the Lesbian and Gay Bereavement Project offering support and advice for gay men, lesbians and their friends and families.
Helpline on 020 7403 5969 from 7pm to 10.30pm, Monday to Friday.

Hospice Information Service

St Christopher's Hospice
51–59 Lawrie Park Road
Sydenham
London
SE26 6DZ

Tel: 020 8778 9252 (Monday–Friday, 8am–5pm,
answerphone at other times)
Fax: 020 8776 9345
Email: his@stchris.ftech.co.uk
http://www.kcl.ac.uk/kis/schools/kcsmd/palliative/his.htm
UK directory of hospices and palliative care services (see web details)
and information for members of the public as well as professionals
caring for people with life–threatening or terminal illness.

Jewish Bereavement Counselling Service
PO Box 6748
London
N3 3BX
Tel: 020 8349 0839
Counselling services for the Jewish faith.

London Bereavement Network
356 Holloway Road
London
N7 6PN
Tel: 020 7700 8134
Fax: 020 7700 8146
Email: infor@bereavement.org.uk
http://www.bereavement.org.uk
Supports and links London bereavement services.

Marie Curie Cancer Care
89 Albert Embankment
London
SE1 7TP
Tel: 020 7599 7777
Fax: 020 7599 7708
Email: info@mariecurie.org.uk
http://www.mariecurie.org.uk
Information about hospices and the availability of night nurses.

Merry Widow

Kate Boydell was widowed at the age of 33 and has written a practical guide for women in her position who need clear, simple advice.

http://www.merrywidow.me.uk

Miscarriage Association

Clayton Hospital
Northgate
Wakefield
WF1 3JF
Tel: 01924 200799
http://www.miscarriageassociation.org.uk
Information and support for those faced with pregnancy loss.

National Association of Bereavement Services

20 Norton Folgate
London
E1 6DB
Tel: 020 7247 1080 (referrals)
020 7247 0617 (admin)
Information about bereavement counselling services in your local area.

National Association of Widows

54–57 Allison Street
Digbeth
Birmingham
B5 5TH
Tel: 0121 643 8348
Information and details of local branches. Contact list for young widows also available.

The Natural Death Centre

6 Blackstock Mews
Blackstock Road
London
N4 2BT
Tel: 020 7359 8391
Fax: 020 7354 3831
Email: rhino@dial.pipex.com
http://www.naturaldeath.org.uk

An educational charity founded in 1991 to parallel the natural childbirth movement. The centre wants to make death and dying an unexceptional topic for daily meditation and conversation. It provides advice and information and acts as a consumers' association. It publishes a wide number of publications, including the invaluable *New Natural Death Handbook*. It offers a helpline (Monday–Friday, during office hours) and can help people arrange DIY, inexpensive and green funerals, supplies living wills, runs courses and offers counselling.

Pagan Federation

BM Box 7097
London
WC1N 3XX
Tel: 01787 238257
Email: President@paganfed.demon.co.uk
http://www.paganfed.demon.co.uk

Information and networking association.

Postal Lending Library

Mary Malcolmson got a number of books together to try and tell her where her son had gone and maybe help other people who were going through what she was going through. See http://www.postallendinglibrary.co.uk or email: postlendlibrary@eastyorkshire.fsnet.co.uk.

React

St Luke's House
270 Sandycombe Road
Kew
Surrey
TW9 3NP
Tel: 020 8940 2575
Fax: 020 8940 2050
Assistance for children with reduced life expectancy.

The Samaritans

PO Box 9090
Stirling
FK8 2SA
National number: 0345 909090
email: jo@smaritans.org or samaritans@anon.twwells.com
http://www.samaritans.org.uk
The primary aim of The Samaritans is to be available at any hour
of the day or night to befriend people who are facing a personal
crisis, including bereavement. Sometimes it is better to talk in
confidence to someone with time to listen, who is not a close
friend or family member. Also see your local phone book.

Stillbirth and Neonatal Death Society (SANDS)

28 Portland Place
London
W1B 1LY
Tel: 020 7436 7940 Admin/publications
Helpline: 020 7436 5881 9.30am–3.30pm, Monday–Friday
Email: support@uk-sands.org
http://www.uk-sands.org
Charity providing support and information for bereaved parents,
whose baby has died at or soon after birth, and their families
and friends. National network of UK groups, telephone helpline,
books and leaflets.

Support after Murder or Manslaughter (SAMM)
Cranmer House
39 Brixton Road
London
SW9 6DZ
Tel: 020 7735 3838
Fax: 020 7735 3900
Email: samm@uk.people.net
http://www.samm.org.uk
Support groups for those affected by murder or manslaughter.

Twins and Multiple Births Association – Bereavement Support Group
Narnott House
309 Chester Road
Little Sutton
Ellesmere Port
CH66 1QQ
Tel: 0151 348 0020
Email: Tamba@information4u.com
http://www.surreyweb.org.uk/Tamba

The Way Foundation
PO Box 74
Penarth
CF64 5ZD
Tel: 02920 711209
Email: info@wayfoundation.org.uk
http://www.wayfoundation.org.uk
Support charity with networking groups and social events for those bereaved under the age of 50.

Victim Support
National Office
Cranmer House
39 Brixton Road
London
SW9 6DZ
Tel: 020 7735 9166
Helpline: 0845 30 30 900
Can put you in touch with local Victim Support schemes to
help victims of crime. Witness Service offers information about
court proceedings.

Voluntary Euthanasia Society
13 Prince of Wales Terrace
London
W8 5PG
Tel: 020 7937 7770
Email: info@ves.org.uk
http://www.ves.org.uk
Formerly Exit, the society who pioneered the Living
Will in the UK.

Winston's Wish
The Clare Burgess Centre
Gloucestershire Royal Hospital
Great Western Road
Gloucester
GL1 3NN
Tel: 01452 394377
Winston's Wish Family Line – 0845 20 30 40 5 (local call rate) –
a national telephone helpline offering guidance and information
– Monday–Friday, 9.30am–5pm.
Email: info@winstonswish.org.uk
http://www.winstonswish.org.uk
Support for bereaved children aged up to 18 and their families

and carers – free to families living in Gloucestershire, UK, but contact if the bereaved family lives outside the country. Charity works closely with children and families to create an atmosphere where they can share their feelings and meet others.

Services include home assessments, residential camp weekends, social activities, support for children when a close family member is dying and a support programme for schools.

War Widows of Great Britain
c/o 11 Chichester Close
Bury St Edmunds
Suffolk
IP33 2LZ
Tel: 0870 2411305
Advice and support for widows of all wars.

Yad b'Yad
c/o Louise Heilbron
8 Grove Avenue
London
N10 2AR
Tel: 020 8444 7134
Email: heilbron@cheerful
Hebrew for Hand in Hand, Yad b'Yad is a Jewish child bereavement project.

PET CHARITIES AND SUPPORT GROUPS

The Cinnamon Trust
Foundry House
Foundry Square
Hayle
Cornwall
TR27 4HE
Tel: 01736 7579000
Cares for pets belonging to the elderly and terminally ill.

People's Dispensary for Sick Animals (PDSA)
Whitechapel Way
Priorslee
Telford
Shropshire
TF2 9DQ
Tel: 0800 591 248

RECOMMENDED
ADC–RELATED WEBSITES

http://www.after-death.com – extensive pages by Bill and Judy Guggenheim focusing on their ADC research.

http://www.adcrf.org – After-Death Communication Research Foundation. ADCRF is dedicated to the ADC experiencers and their search for meaning and understanding in the loss of their loved one.

http://www.ndeweb.com – based on knowledge and meaning of NDEs.

http://www.nderf.org – The thorough work of the Near-Death Experience Research Foundation.

http://www.datadiwan.de/SciMedNet/library/articlesN75+/N76P arnia_nde.htm – 'Near Death Experiences in Cardiac Arrest and the Mystery of Consciousness' is a thorough article by Dr Sam Parnia outlining his detailed and fascinating research into NDEs amid cardiac arrest victims and data I really would strongly recommend you delve into if NDEs interest you.

http://www.oberf.org – The Out-of-Body Experience Research Foundation which is devoted to these NDE-like experiences, spontaneous out-of-body experiences and spiritually transformative events.

FICTIONAL ADCs
IN MOVIES[55]

Alice – a Woody Allen comedy starring Mia Farrow, Joe Mantegna and William Hurt (1991). Married 15 years to a very wealthy man, Alice is a vaguely unhappy and shallow Manhattanite who's filled with romantic fantasies.

She has three encounters with her old boyfriend, Eddie (Alec Baldwin), who died in an automobile accident 20 years earlier. And her deceased mother (Gwen Verdon) also appears once.

Always – starring Richard Dreyfuss, Holly Hunter and John Goodman (1989). Pete, a pilot for the forest fire service, dies in a mid-air explosion. Later, his co-worker and girlfriend, Dorinda, recklessly flies off to rescue six firefighters who are trapped on the ground. Although she is successful, her plane crashes into a lake, and Pete intervenes to save her from drowning.

Arthur 2 – On the Rocks – starring Dudley Moore, Liza Minnelli and John Gielgud (1988). Arthur, an immature alcoholic, loses his fortune and his wife. Hobson, his deceased butler, makes a full appearance and confronts him for wallowing in self-pity and giving up. This powerful ADC causes Arthur to hit bottom, cease drinking and turn his life around.

Da – starring Barnard Hughes and Martin Sheen (1988). When his foster-father dies in Ireland, Charlie flies to his funeral and stays on to settle his estate. His da (dad) appears to him frequently and they have numerous conversations. This film presents an imaginative collage of ADCs, memories and flashbacks.

Field of Dreams – starring Kevin Costner, Amy Madigan and James Earl Jones (1989). Ray hears 'The Voice' and builds a baseball field on his farm in Iowa as an act of faith. Ray's deceased father, John, comes back as a young man to have a baseball catch – and a healing reunion – with his son. Shoeless Joe Jackson and other dead ballplayers also come to the field.

Ghost – starring Patrick Swayze, Demi Moore and Whoopi Goldberg (1990). Sam is shot and killed during an apparent mugging in New York City. He learns that his girlfriend, Molly, is in great danger, and he seeks to protect her by communicating through a reluctant psychic, Oda Mae.

The main ADC occurs at the end of the movie when Molly is able to see and communicate with Sam, and they kiss before he goes into the Light.

The Heavenly Kid – starring Lewis Smith, Jason Gedrick and Jane Kaczmarek (1985). Bobby fulfils his assignment as a guardian angel to a teenage boy. He also makes an appearance to his former girlfriend, Emily, to complete his unfinished business with her. He tells Emily that he'll always be with her.

Kiss Me Goodbye – starring Sally Field, James Caan and Jeff Bridges (1982). In this romantic farce, Kay, a widow of three years, finds her plans to marry her fiancé, Rupert, are complicated by the presence of her charming and egotistical deceased husband, Jolly. Only she can see and communicate with him.

The Lion King – this animated Walt Disney movie stars the voices of Matthew Broderick, Jeremy Irons and James Earl Jones (1994). Mufasa, the king of the jungle and the father of young Simba, is killed by his ambitious brother, Scar. However, Simba believes he alone was the cause of his father's death and becomes an exile due to his guilt.

Years later, Simba sees his deceased father in an ADC vision. Mufasa reminds his grown son of his true responsibility. He urges Simba to return and claim his rightful position as the ruler of the kingdom, thereby deposing Scar who has assumed all power for himself.

A Midsummer Night's Sex Comedy – Woody Allen wrote, directed and stars in this romantic comedy in which three couples share a summer weekend together in the country, around 1900 – also starring Mia Farrow and Jose Ferrer (1982).

One of the men, Leopold, is a pompous professor and an avowed atheist. However, when he dies after making love, his soul is seen as a small ball of light as he bids a joyful farewell to his five friends.

The Phantom – starring Billy Zane, Treat Williams, Kristy Swanson and James Remar and based upon the popular comic-strip hero (1996). The Phantom's father (Patrick McGoohan), who was killed by being stabbed in the back, makes three full appearances to his son, which include one-way and two-way communication. One of the occasions occurs during a taxi-cab ride in New York City, though the driver doesn't see or hear his extra passenger.

The Star Wars Trilogy – starring Mark Hamil, Harrison Ford and Carrie Fisher – with Alec Guinness.

Star Wars (1977). Ben (Obi-Wan) Kenobi, a Jedi Knight, befriends young Luke Skywalker and teaches him about The Force. After he is slain, Obi-Wan becomes even more powerful than when he was alive. He directs Luke to use The Force while he attacks the Empire's battle station in his X-wing fighter.

The Empire Strikes Back (1980). When Luke is lost and freezing to death on an icy planet, Obi-Wan makes a full appearance to give him a message and provide encouragement. Later, he appears to both Luke and Yoda, the Jedi Master, to give Luke an important warning.

Return of the Jedi (1983). Obi-Wan appears to Luke after Yoda dies, explains who Darth Vader is, and reveals that Luke has a twin sister. Obi-Wan, Yoda and Luke's father, Anakin Skywalker, make full appearances together to Luke during the celebration of the defeat of the evil Empire.

Some Girls – starring Patrick Dempsey and Jennifer Connelly (1989). In this unusual comedy, an American college student spends his Christmas vacation with his girlfriend and her eccentric family in Quebec. He befriends her dying granny (Lila Kedrova) and brings flowers to her tomb on Christmas Day.

There he encounters a mysterious young woman who disappears. Later, he identifies her from an old portrait – a picture of Granny in the prime of her life.

Topper – starring Cary Grant and Constance Bennett (1937). After dying in an auto accident, George and Marion Kerby realise they must perform a good deed. They help Cosmo Topper, a stuffy banker, and his prudish wife to be more playful and improve their marriage. The Kerbys appear and communicate many times to the Toppers and others.

This popular comedy inspired two movie sequels and a TV show, and many other films and TV programmes have been based on a similar premise.

Truly, Madly, Deeply – an English film starring Juliet Stevenson and Alan Rickman (1991). Nina is a deeply bereaved widow after her husband, Jamie, dies suddenly from an illness.

At first, she is comforted when he returns to her in a lifelike way, but his presence soon becomes more of a burden than a joy. Eventually, a new romance enters her life and she asks Jamie to leave her for good.

2010 – starring Roy Scheider (1984). In *2001: A Space Odyssey* (1968), astronaut David Bowman died while exploring the huge black monolith near Jupiter. In this sequel, he appears on earth to his former wife, Betty, on a TV set, and contacts his aged mother just before she dies.

He also appears to Dr Heywood Floyd aboard the spaceship *Discovery* to give him an urgent warning.

FICTIONAL ADCs IN
NOVELS AND PLAYS[55]

AFTER-DEATH COMMUNICATIONS OFTEN appear in works of fiction, too – in novels, theatre plays, movies and television shows. However, we usually see ADCs without acknowledging them for what they are. We regard them as mere 'literary devices', creative inventions of imaginative minds, that are used as vehicles to assist in the telling of a story.

But why do ADCs appear so consistently? What is their source of inspiration? Are they possibly more than just fiction?

Angels of September, by Andrew M Greeley (1986) – Anne Reilly is a beautiful and intelligent woman in her 50s who operates her own art gallery in Chicago. Dick Murray, her high school sweetheart, was killed on his first day of combat in Germany during World War II. He makes six full appearances to her during the next 40 years.

The most recent one occurs at a beach in full sunlight when Dick sits down beside Anne, touches her face with his hand and winks at her before departing. To Anne, he is 'as real as anyone on the beach'.

Another of Father Greeley's novels, **Rite of Spring**, contains detailed accounts of two full appearances a deceased wife makes to her living husband, Brendan Ryan.

Blithe Spirit, by Noel Coward (1941) – Both of Charles's deceased wives, first Elvira and later Ruth, unexpectedly come back and stay on in his home. He's the only one who can see and communicate with them.

Their eternal triangle creates great friction in this farcical British comedy. The situation is further complicated by Madame Arcati, a well–intentioned but deluded medium, who adds great spirit to this madcap play.

Bluebirds, by David W Frasure (1978) – in this metaphysical love story, Kris McDaniels dramatically enters the lives of Allison Haynes and her family members. Kris and Allison quickly develop a very loving, spiritual relationship, but he dies soon afterwards in a construction accident.

Kris appears to Allison in a sleep-state ADC and assures her he will always be close by to help her in all ways possible, if she will only remember to ask for his assistance.

Captains and the Kings, by Taylor Caldwell (1972) – fleeing famine and English persecution in Ireland, Daniel Armagh emigrates to America. He sends for his family several months later, and his pregnant wife, Moira, sails steerage class for New York with their two sons. Shortly after giving birth to a daughter, Moira is severely ill and sees Daniel, joyfully stretching her arms out to him before she dies. She had no way of knowing her husband had died of lung fever two months earlier. Though this is an ADC, it's more properly classified as 'a death-bed vision'.

Carousel, by Richard Rodgers and Oscar Hammerstein II (1945) – in this hit musical, Billy Bigelow, the barker for the carousel, loses his job, marries Julie Jordan and learns he will be a father soon.

Out of desperation for money, he participates in an unsuccessful robbery and takes his life just before he's captured.

Fifteen years later, Billy is allowed to return to earth for one day to complete his unfinished business. He makes a full appearance to his daughter, Louise, who was born after he died. Julie senses his presence and sees him for an instant.

At his daughter's graduation, Billy speaks to Louise and Julie, inspiring them, as everyone sings the hope-filled song 'You'll Never Walk Alone'.

A Christmas Carol, by Charles Dickens (1843) – this story contains the best–known example of a fictional ADC in English literature. Cold-hearted Ebenezer Scrooge is visited by his former business partner, Jacob Marley, who has died seven years earlier.

Marley's body is transparent and encircled by a chain of money boxes and other valuables. He must wander through the world, earthbound, for having valued money more than mankind.

Marley returns to tell Scrooge that he has a chance to escape a similar fate, and will be visited by three spirits who will help him.

A Death in the Family, by James Agee (1938) – one evening, Jay Flollet is killed instantly in a single-car accident. Hours later, his widow, Mary, her aunt, Hannah, her brother, Andrew, and her mother, Catherine, all sense Jay's presence while they are mourning his death together. Only her very rational father, Joel, doesn't feel the presence of his deceased son-in-law, and he dismisses their experiences as hallucinations. Shortly afterwards, Mary and Hannah sense Jay's presence a second time, when he returns to visit his two young children, Rufus and Catherine. And finally they all have a group discussion of what they sensed and felt.

At the end of this novel, Andrew tells his nephew, Rufus, that as they were lowering his father's body into the ground at the cemetery, 'a perfectly magnificent butterfly settled on the coffin'. Just as the casket touched the bottom of the grave, the sun came out and the butterfly 'flew up out of that hole in the ground, straight up into the sky, so high I couldn't even see him any more'. And he concludes by saying, 'If there are any such things as miracles, then that's surely miraculous.'

The Family Circus, by Bil Keane (continuous) – this popular cartoon appears in the daily and Sunday comics section of many American newspapers. It occasionally features Jeffy's grandfather, Al, who has died. Al is sitting on a bed in front of his widow, Florence, as she's talking to him (19/2/89); he's seen in Heaven listening to what his grandson is saying about him (20/8/89); and he's seen in the background when Jeffy tells his father that he heard his granddad say, 'G'night, Little Buddy, and God bless you' (12/9/93).

Al is sitting on a couch with his left arm around Florence and his right hand holding her hands (23/6/91); and he assists her when she's lost while driving her car (5/4/92). And there are many more recent ones too.

Fiddler on the Roof, by Joseph Stein (1964) – Golde and Tevye's young daughter, Tzeitel, has been promised in marriage to the wealthy butcher, Lazar Wolf. But Tzeitel wants to marry the poor tailor, Motel Kamzoil.

Without Golde's knowledge, Tevye gives Tzeitel his permission to wed Motel. Now he must inform his wife and face her wrath. He manipulates Golde by pretending to have a sleep-state ADC in which her deceased grandmother returns to say that Tzeitel should marry the tailor.

This 'dream' is usually acted out on stage in their bedroom. Golde accepts the guidance from her grandmother who has been dead for 30 years and allows her daughter to wed the tailor.

Audiences of this hit Broadway play accept this presentation of an ADC as a plausible event. Unfortunately, the movie version places this scene in a cemetery and portrays it in a ghostly manner.

The Golden Bird, by Hans Stop (1987) – 11-year–old Daniel is terminally ill with cancer and confined to a hospital. His deceased father visits him to calm his son's fears and remove his pain. When Daniel makes his transition, his dad comes to takes his hand and they leave together.

Gump & Co, by Winston Groom (1995) – in this sequel to the best-selling book and blockbuster movie, *Forrest Gump*, Forrest has a series of visual ADCs with Jenny, his deceased wife, who gives him practical advice when he needs it most. And even his son, little Forrest, has an ADC with his deceased mother, though he calls it 'a dream'.

Hamlet, by William Shakespeare (circa 1600) – in this very evidential ADC, it's believed that King Hamlet of Denmark suffered an accidental death from being bitten by a snake. Now deceased and wearing a suit of armour, he makes a full appearance to his young son, Prince Hamlet.

He reveals to his son that he was murdered by his brother, Claudius (Hamlet's uncle), who poured a poison into his ear while he was asleep in an orchard. Claudius's motive was to marry Gertrude, the Queen of Denmark (Hamlet's mother), and thereby become the new King of Denmark himself.

King Hamlet orders his son to avenge his death, and young Hamlet swears to do so. But first he must prove to himself, beyond any doubt, that his father has told him the truth.

King Hamlet makes a second, brief appearance to his son later in the play, to remind him of his pledge.

The House of the Spirits, by Isabel Allende (1982) – this international best-seller recounts three generations of a wealthy family in Chile. Ferula makes a full appearance in front of five people, touches her sister-in-law, Clara, and kisses her on the forehead – before anyone knows she has died.

Later, Esteban sees Clara, his deceased wife, frequently and hears her laughter. Clara also appears to her granddaughter, Alba, and gives her a reason to live when she is imprisoned. This book shows how commonplace and accepted ADCs are in other cultures.

Illusions, by Richard Bach (1977) – after his friend, Donald William Shimoda, is killed in the cockpit of his plane by a shotgun blast, Richard meets him again in a sleep-state ADC. Don continues Richard's messiah training, and he promises they can meet again whenever Richard has a problem and needs his help. Don also suggests that Richard should consider writing a book – this book – about their adventures together.

Les Misérables, by Alain Boublil and Claude-Michel Schönberg, based on the novel by Victor Hugo, music by Claude-Michel Schönberg and lyrics by Herbert Kretzmer (1990) – at the end of this very successful play, as Jean Valjean is dying, two women who had died earlier, Fantine and Eponine, come to escort him to the light. They are joined in the background by all those who had died at the barricades.

Littlejohn, by Howard Owen (1993) – Littlejohn McCain, a farmer in rural North Carolina, is 82 years old and awaiting death. As he is actually dying, he sees many of his deceased loved ones who have come to assist and welcome him as he makes his transition. These include his parents; his wife, Sara; his brother, Lafe, who died at 19 from an accidental gunshot wound years earlier; his other brother, Lex; and his two sisters, Century and Connie.

The Little Match Girl, from Hans Christian Andersen's *Fairy Tales*, selected and illustrated by Lisbeth Zwerger, and translated by Anthea Bell (nineteenth century) – alone, without money, starving and freezing to death on the streets of a big city, the little girl lights her unsold matches for warmth.

Her deceased grandmother makes a full appearance to her, and when the little girl dies, they soar together to Heaven where

the little match girl no longer feels any more hunger, cold or pain.
Rainbow in the Mist, by Phyllis A Whitney (1989) – during this
romance-mystery, Donny Mitchell, age six or seven, has an ADC
with his mother, Deirdre, who died in a fall. She appears to
Donny and reassures him she is happy, tells him he shouldn't cry
for her, and that he must learn to let her go.

Remember the Secret, by Elisabeth Kübler-Ross (1982) – Suzy and
Peter are children who are best friends with each other. They are
also close to two 'imaginary playmates', Theresa and Willy.

When Peter dies, Suzy sees him with Theresa and Willy and
realises all three of them are her guardian angels. She can also hear
Peter when he speaks to her.

The Return of Peter Grimm, by David Belasco (1911) – in this popular
Broadway play, Peter Grimm, the family patriarch, dies suddenly
from a heart ailment. He returns ten days after his death to correct
a mistake he made while alive.

He seeks to release his foster-daughter, Catherine, from her
promise to marry his nephew, Frederik. Only William, aged eight,
can hear (and later, see) Peter, though several people are affected
by his presence.

This play was inspired by an ADC David Belasco had with his
mother who made a full appearance to her son kissed him, and
spoke to him.

Saint Joan, by George Bernard Shaw (1923) – during the final
scene of this play, it's 1456, 25 years after Joan of Arc was burned
at the stake by the Church for heresy, witchcraft and sorcery.

Portrayed as a sleep-state ADC, Joan and others make full
appearances to King Charles the Seventh of France in his
bedroom. Joan learns the Church has exonerated her of her
crimes – the first major step towards canonising her as a saint
in 1920.

A Simple Heart, by Gustave Flaubert in his book written in French, *Three Tales*, (1877) translated by Walter J Cobb – Madame Aubain became a widow when her husband died in 1809. A few years later, her young daughter, Virginie, dies of pneumonia and Mme Aubain is heartbroken. Shortly afterwards, she sees her husband and daughter standing next to each other in her garden.

Stonewords, by Pam Conrad (1990) – soon after Zoe, aged four, begins living with her grandparents, she meets a deceased young girl, Zoe Louise, who becomes her best friend. Zoe Louise had lived in the same house over 100 years earlier.

Several years later, Zoe travels back in time to protect Zoe Louise from dying in a fire on her eleventh birthday. This story is an excellent example of a child who has an 'imaginary playmate'.

Tilly, by Frank E Peretti (1988) – in this short novel, Kathy has a long out-of-body ADC and visits a lovely young girl who lives in another world. She learns this child, Tilly, is her daughter – whom she has never known because of the abortion she had nine years earlier.

During their extended reunion, Kathy receives forgiveness from Tilly and from Jesus. When she awakens, Kathy is healed of her guilt and filled with peace in her heart.

Walk in My Soul, by Lucia St Clair Robson (1985) – this historical novel portrays the life of Tiana Rogers, a member of the Cherokee who are forced to leave their home in Tennessee and move westward along the infamous Trail of Tears. Her young daughter, Gabriel, dies of yellow fever.

Later, when Tiana is feeling lonely and questioning her life, she feels the presence of her deceased grandmother, Ulisi, and hears her voice in her head. Ulisi tells Tiana, 'You are never alone, granddaughter ... Gabriel is here with me. We are not far from you.'

Whalesong — A Novel About the Greatest and Deepest of Beings, by Robert Siegel (1981) — Hruna, the young leader of a pod of humpback whales, has an ADC vision from which he receives teachings from Hralekana, a white humpback who was the spiritual leader of the pod. This is a very well-written spiritual fable.

When You Can Walk on Water, Take the Boat, by John Harricharan (1986) — John has an out-of-body ADC with his father that is very reassuring and joyful. As the two men talk at length, his father explains why he died and shares various aspects of life after death. This account is based on an actual ADC experience the author had with his father.

John has written a sequel, *Morning Has Been All Night Coming* (1991), in which he and his children have ADCs with his deceased wife, Mardai

ENDNOTES

1   Levine, Art. 1987. *Mystics on Main Street, US News & World Report* (9 Feb): 67–69
2   Guggenheim, Bill and Judy. *Hello from Heaven!* (Thorsons, 1996): 15
3   Marris, P, *Widows and Their Families* (London, RKP 1958)
4   Parkes, CM, *Bereavement and Mental Illness* (*British Journal of Medical Psychology*, 38, 1) (1965)
5   Adapted from http://paranormal.about.com/library/weekly/aa021901a.htm
6   Davies, Douglas, *Death, Ritual and Belief*
7   Cleiren, M PhD, *Adaptation after Bereavement* (Leiden: Leiden University Press, 1991) 129
8   Moody, Raymond, *Reunions* (Warner Books, 1996) Widows were selected for these studies simply because women tend to outlive men – there are therefore more widows making them more accessible for study.
9   Finucane, RC, *Appearances of the Dead: A Cultural History of Ghosts* (Junction Books: London, 1982) p. 223
10 Adapted from John Hooper, *Dialogue with the Dead is Feasible* (London *Observer* Service)

11 Department of Sociology & Anthropology, Trinity University, Texas

12 Information and chart taken from http://www.trinity.edu/mkearl/spirits.html

13 Wills-Brandon, C, *One Last Hug Before I Go: The Mystery and Meaning of Death-Bed Visions* (2000) HCI Publications

14 *Numinis* No. 12 April 1993

15 This article was published in the *Cincinnati Enquirer* on 5 October 1993 and was written by Adam Weintraub

16 *Miami Herald*: DREAM TICKET – LOTTO WINNER: DEAD DAUGHTER TOLD ME TO PLAY (7 July 1988)

17 Melvin Morse – *Death-Related Visions and Healing Grief* taken from: http://www.death-dying.com/articles/visions.html

18 Long, J.P. and Long, J.A. After-Death Communication Research Foundation (www. adcrf.org)

19 Taken from http://www.gqmagazine.co.uk/Daily_News/default.asp?nxtStory=1002, 13 August 2001

20 As reported in *Theodore Roosevelt – A Life* by Nathan Miller, this date would also have been the 70th birthday of the President's deceased father.

21 With thanks to Craig Hamilton-Parker. For further accounts see *What to do When You Are Dead* (Stirling Publications 2001) and *The Psychic Case Book* (Stirling Publications 1999)

22 George S. Patton, Jr, *Before The Colors Fade*

23 This article was published by the *Miami Sun-Sentinel* on March 3, 1998 and was written by Donna Pazdera

24 The ABC interview was the first of a four-part discussion in which McCartney discussed his marriage, children and his relationship with Lennon. *Info Beat*, 1 May 2001

25 With thanks to Craig Hamilton-Parker. For further accounts see *What To Do When You Are Dead* (Stirling Publications 2001) and *The Psychic Case Book* (Stirling Publications 1999)

26 *Daily Star*, 13 December 2002

27 This article was published in the *Asbury Park Press* on 10

October 1996 and was written by the Associated Press

[28] Guggenheim, B and J, *Hello from Heaven!*, Chapter 1

[29] Sally Jessy Raphael syndicated (1 December 1989) – Topic: 'I Was Too Young To Lose My Wife'

[30] Taken from http://www.canoe.ca/LifewiseHeartSoulwise00/0524_death.html, 24 May 2000.

[31] *Observer* magazine 18-25. *Dispatches* – Article by Emily Yoffe, 12/1/03

[32] *Bereavement* magazine: *Matt's Butterfly* by Bob Pano (May/June, 1994)

[33] For further information see the findings as described in Soloman, G and J, *The Schole Experiment: Scientific Evidence for Life after Death* (Piatkus; London, 1999)

[34] This article was published in the *National Enquirer* on 8 October 1996 and was written by Stan Oliver.

[35] Long, J.P., and Long, J.A. (2003) After Death Communication Research Foundation (www.adcrf.org) Wendy A's ADC (http://www.adcrf.org/wendy_a's_adc.htm) (With Permission)

[36] Long, J.P., and Long, J.A. (2003). After Death Communication Research Foundation (www.adcrf.org). Steve P's ADC (http://www.adcrf.org/steve_p's_adc.htm) (With Permission)

[37] *Hollywood And The Supernatural* by Sherry Hansen-Steiger and Brad Steiger

[38] *GQ* magazine, article by Craig Hamilton-Parker

[39] With thanks to Craig Hamilton-Parker. For further accounts see *What To Do When You Are Dead* (Stirling Publications 2001) and *The Psychic Case Book* (Stirling Publications 1999)

[40] It was a prospective clinical study of 10 hospitals, 344 cardiac patients, with 2- and 8-year follow-ups

[41] 12-15-01, The *Lancet Medical Journal*

[42] For more information see, amongst others: Dr Raymond A Moody, *Life after Life* (1975), *Reflections on Life after Life* (1977); K Osis and E Haraldson, *At the Hour of Death* (1977); Prof Kenneth Ring, *Life at Death* (1980); Dr Michael B Sabom,

Recollections of Death (1982); Dr Elizabeth Kubler-Ross (no books published on this subject, but many lectures given which can be downloaded from the internet); Dr Fred Schoonmaker (no books published, but said to have recorded 1,400 NDEs among 2,300 near-death cases – *Reader's Digest*, August 1981); The IANDS (International Association for Near-Death Studies); Near-Death Research Federation.

[43] Monist: the nature of man is singular in dimension, that is, a purely natural being of an electro-chemical nature

[44] http://www.apc.net/drdianne/1.htm – Website of Dianne Morrissey PhD, 9/4/01

[45] For more on this see Heathcote-James, E, *Seeing Angels* (Blake Publishing, Aug 2001)

[46] http://www.apc.net/drdianne/3.htm, 9/4/01

[47] Leroy Kattein as outlined on his site http://www.ndeweb.com/wildcard

[48] Davies, Douglas, *Death, Ritual and Belief* (Cassell, London 1997), p168

[49] *Radio Times* – 27 April 1991, along with an extensive documentary.

[50] For detailed results and analysis of this survey see Davies, Douglas, *Death, Ritual and Belief* (Cassell, London 1997), pp169–172.

[51] Davies, Douglas, *Death, Ritual and Belief* (Cassell, London 1997), pp170-1.

[52] Taken with permission from http://www.adcrf.org

[53] Davies, Douglas, *Death, Ritual and Belief* (Cassell, London 1997), p172.

[54] Louis LaGrand, www.anotherreality.com

[55] Resources that include ADCs, compiled by The ADC Project at: http://www.after-death.com, with permission

[56] Resources that include ADCs, compiled by The ADC Project at: http://www.after-death.com, with permission

BIBLIOGRAPHY AND SUGGESTED FURTHER READING

As there are few books actually written on ADCs at present, this list mainly comprises books that contain discussions on related topics such as spiritualism, near-death experiences, spiritual healing, reincarnation, psychic development and para-psychological research on survival as well as several biographies and memoirs of mediums and psychics.

Abbott, David Phelps, *Behind the Scenes with the Mediums* (Chicago, The Open Court Publishing Co., 1907)

Almeder, Robert, *Beyond Death: Evidence for Life After Death* (Springfield, Illinois, Charles C. Thomas, Publisher, 1987)

Altea, Rosemary, *You Own the Power: Stories and Exercises to Inspire and Unleash the Force Within* (New York, Eagle Brook-William Morrow and Company, 2000)

Altea, Rosemary, *The Eagle and the Rose Proud Spirit* (New York, Eagle Brook-William Morrow and Company, 1997), *The Eagle and the Rose: A Remarkable True Story* (New York, Warner Books, 1995)

Anderson, George, and Andrew Barone *Lessons from the Light:*

Extraordinary Messages of Comfort and Hope from the Other Side (New York, G. P. Putnam's Sons, 1999)

Archer, Fred, *Crime and the Psychic World* (New York, William Morrow & Co., 1969)

Aron, Elaine N., *The Highly Sensitive Person: How to Thrive When the World Overwhelms You* (New York Broadway Books, 1997)
Atwater, P, *Beyond the Light*

Auerbach, Loyd, *ESP, Hauntings and Poltergeists: A Parapsychologist's Handbook* (New York, Warner Books, 1986)

Barbanell, Maurice, *I Hear A Voice: A Biography of E. G. Fricker the Healer* (London, Spiritualist Press, 1962)

Barbanell, Sylvia, *Some Discern Spirits: The Mediumship of Estelle Roberts* (London, Psychic Press Limited, 1944) *When A Child Dies* (London, Psychic Press Ltd., 1942)

Bardens, Dennis, *Psychic Animals: A Fascinating Investigation of Paranormal Behavior* (New York: Henry Holt, 1987)

Bernstein, Morey, *The Search for Bridey Murphy*. (Garden City, New York, Doubleday & Co., 1956)

Besant, Annie, and C. W. Leadbeater, *Thought-Forms* (Wheaton, Illinois, Quest Book-The Theosophical Publishing House, 1971). First published in 1901 by the Theosophical Publishing House, Adyar, Madrar, India.

Blackmore, Susan, *Dying to Live*.

Bloom, William, *Psychic Protection: Creating Positive Energies for People and Places* (New York, Simon & Schuster, 1996) *The Boy Who Saw True*, With an Introduction, Afterword and Notes by Cyril Scott (Great Britain, The C. W. Daniel Company Limited, 1953)

Braude, Ann, *Radical Spirits: Spiritualism and Women's Rights in Nineteenth-Century America* (Boston, Beacon Press, 1989)

Brinkley, Dannion, with Paul Perry, *Saved by the Light* (New York, Villard Books, 1994)

Brown, Rosemary, *Immortals by My Side* (Chicago, Henry Regnery Company, 1974) *Unfinished Symphonies: Voices from the Beyond* (New York, William Morrow and Company, 1971)

Browne, Mary T., *Mary T. Reflects on the Other Side: A Compelling Vision of the Afterlife* (New York: Fawcett Columbine, 1994). [A paperback edition of this book has been published under the new title *Life After Death* (New York, Ivy Books, 1994.]

Buckland, Raymond, *Doors to Other Worlds: A Practical Guide to Communicating with Spirits* (St. Paul, Minnesota, Llewellyn Publications, 1994)

Budden, Albert, *Electric UFOs: Fireballs, Electromagnetics, and Abnormal States* (London, Blandford, 1998)

Budzynski, Thomas, *Tuning in on the Twilight Zone* from *Psychology Today* (August 1977)

Carrington, Hereward. *The Physical Phenomena of Spiritualism: Fraudulent and Genuine – Being a Brief Account of the Most Important Historical Phenomena; A Criticism of Their Evidential Value, and a Complete Exposition of the Methods Employed in Fraudulently Reproducing the Same* (New York, Dodd, Mead & Company, 1920) (Copyright 1907 by Herbert B. Turner & Co.)

Cerminara, Gina, *Many Mansions: 'The Edgar Cayce Story of Reincarnation'* (New York, New American Library, 1978)

Cerutti, Edwina, *Olga Worrall: Mystic with Healing Hands* (New York, Harper & Row, 1975)

Chambers, Paul, *Paranormal People: The Famous, the Infamous and the Supernatural* (1998)

Chase, Warren, *Forty Years on the Spiritual Rostrum* (Boston, Colby & Rich, Publishers, 1888)

Christopher, Milbourne, *Mediums, Mystics & the Occult: New Revelations about the Psychics and Their Secrets* (New York, Thomas Y. Crowell Company, 1975)

Cleiren, M. PhD., *Adaptation after Bereavement* (Leiden, Leiden University Press, 1991)

Cockell, Jenny. *Across Time and Death: A Mother's Search for Her Past Life Children* (New York, Fireside–Simon & Schuster, 1994)

Conan Doyle, Arthur, *The History of Spiritualism* (New York, Arno Press, 1975). First published in 1926 by George H. Doran Company. *The Wanderings of a Spiritualist* (Berkeley, California, Ronin Publishing, 1988). First published in 1921 by George H. Doran Company.

Concar, David, *Out of Sight into Mind in New Scientist*, 5 September 1998 (ICI Press) pp. 38–41.

Cook, Cecil M, *The Voice Triumphant: The Revelations of a Medium* (New York, Alfred A. Knopf, 1931)

Cooke, Grace, *The New Mediumship* (Liss, Hampshire, England, The White Eagle Publishing Trust, 1965)

Costa, Joseph, *Primal Legacy: Thinking for the 21st Century* (Solana Beach, California, Better Life Books, 1995)

Cowan, Tom, *The Book of Seance: How to Reach Out to the Next World* (Chicago, Contemporary Books, 1994)

Crenshaw, James, *Telephone Between Worlds* (Marina Del Ray, California, DeVorss & Co., 1950)

Crookall, Robert, *The Study and Practice of Astral Projection* (New Hyde Park, New York, University Books, 1966)

Davis, Andrew Jackson, *Beyond the Valley; A Sequel to The Magic Staff: An Autobiography* (Boston, Colby & Rich, 1985)
The Magic Staff: An Autobiography (Rochester, New York, The Austin Publishing Co., 1910) First published in New York in 1857 by J. S. Brown & Co.

Davies, Douglas, *Death, Ritual and Belief* (London, Cassell, 1997)

Dossey, Larry, *Be Careful What You Pray For ... You Just Might Get It* (San Francisco, HarperSanFrancisco, 1997)

Doyle, Sir Arthur Conan, *History of Spiritualism* (1926)

Doyle, Sir Arthur Conan (ed.) *Life and Mission of Home – Scotland and America, DD Home, His Life and Mission: Mme Dunglas Home* (Trench, Trunber and Co Ltd, London, 1921)

Dresser, Horatio W. (Editor.) *The Quimby Manuscripts*. Secaucus (New Jersey, The Citadel Press, 1976). (Originally published in 1921 by Thomas Y. Crowell Co., New York).

Druffel, Ann, and Armand Marcotte, *The Psychic and the Detective* (Norfolk, Virginia, Hampton Roads Publishing Company, 1983)

Eadie, Betty J., with Curtis Taylor. *Embraced by the Light* (Carson City, Nevada, Gold Leaf Press, 1992)

Eckersley, Glennyce S., *Angels and Miracles* (Rider Books, London, 1997)

Eckersley, Glennyce, *Saved by the Angels* (Rider Books, London, 2002)

Eckersley, Glennyce, *Teen Angel* (Rider Books, London, 2003)

Edward, John, *One Last Time: A Psychic Medium Speaks to Those We Have Loved and Lost* (New York, Berkley Books, 1998)

Edwards, Harry, *Thirty Years a Spiritual Healer* (London, Herbert Jenkins, 1968)

Elsaesser Valarino, Evelyn, *On the Other Side of Life: Exploring the Phenomenon of the Near-Death Experience*. Translated by Michelle Herzig Escobar (New York, Insight Books-Plenum Press, 1997)

Fearheiley, Don, *Angels Among Us* (Avon Books, 1993)

Feilding, Everard, *Sittings with Eusapia Palladino & Other Studies* (New Hyde Park,)

Fenwick, Peter and Fenwick, Elizabeth, *The Truth in the Light: An Investigation of over 300 Near-Death Experiences* (BCA by arrangement with Headline, London, 1995, New York, University Books, 1963)

Finucane, RC, *Appearances of the Dead: A Cultural History of Ghosts* (Junction Books, London, 1982)

Fisher, Joe, *The Case for Reincarnation Preface*, by His Holiness the

Dalai Lama (Toronto, William Collins and Sons, 1984)

Flint, Leslie, *Voices in the Dark: My Life as a Medium* (Indianapolis/New York, The Bobbs-Merrill Company, 1971)

Ford, Arthur, *Unknown but Known: My Adventure into the Meditative Dimension* (New York, Harper & Row, Publishers, 1968)

Ford, Arthur, with Margueritte Harmon Bro., *Nothing So Strange: The Autobiography of Arthur Ford* (New York, Harper & Brothers, 1958)

Fodor, Nandor, *Between Two Worlds*. West Nyack (New York, Parker Publishing Company, 1964)

Fortune, Dion, *Psychic Self-Defence: A Study in Occult Pathology and Criminality* (New York, Samuel Weiser, first published in 1930)

Garrett, Eileen J., *Many Voices: The Autobiography of a Medium* (New York, G. P. Putnam's Sons, 1968)

Fox, Matthew and Sheldrake, Rupert, *The Physics of Angels: Exploring the Realm Where Science and Physics Meet* (HarperSanFrancisco, 1996) *Adventures in the Supernormal: A Personal Memoir* (New York, Garrett Publications, 1949)

Goldsmith, Barbara, *Other Powers: The Age of Suffrage, Spiritualism, and the Scandalous Victoria Woodhull* (New York, Knopf, 1998)

Grant, Rob, *The Place We Call Home: Exploring the Soul's Existence after Death* (ARE Press)
Guald, Alan, *Mediumship and Survival* (Heinemann, 1982)

Gross, Richard D, *Psychology: The Science of Mind and Behaviour* – 2nd

Edition (Hodder and Stoughton, London 1993 – 5th imprint)

Guggenheim, Bill and Guggenheim, Judy, *Hello from Heaven!* (Harper Collins Press, London, 1996)

Guiley, Rosemary Ellen, *Harper's Encyclopedia of Mystical & Paranormal Experience* (San Francisco, HarperSanFrancisco, 1991)

Gurvis, Sandra, *Way Stations to Heaven: 50 Sites All Across America Where You Can Experieince the Miraculous* (New York, Macmillan, 1996)

Hamilton-Parker, Craig, *The Psychic Case Book* (Stirling Publications, 1999)

Hamilton-Parker, Craig, *What To Do When You Are Dead* (Stirling Publications, 2001)

Harlow, S. Ralph, *A Life After Death* (Garden City, New York, Doubleday & Company, 1961)

Head, Joseph, and S. L. Cranston, *Reincarnation: The Phoenix Fire Mystery – An East–West Dialogue on Death and Rebirth from the Worlds of Religion, Science, Psychology, Philosophy, Art, and Literature, and from Great Thinkers of the Past and Present* (New York, Julian Press/Crown Publishers, 1977)

Head, Joseph, and S. L. Cranston, *Reincarnation: An East–West Anthology, Including Quotations from the World's Religions & from over 400 Western Thinkers* (Wheaton, Illinois, The Theosophical Publishing House, 1968). First edition 1961 published by The Julian Press, Inc.

Heywood, Rosalind, *ESP: A Personal Memoir,* (New York, E. P. Dutton & Co., 1964)

Hill, Douglas, and Pat Williams, *The Supernatural* (New York, Hawthorn Books. (Copyright 1965 by Aldus Books Limited, London.)

Ibsen, Henrik, *Ghost.*

Iverson, Jeffrey, *In Search of the Dead: A Scientific Investigation of Evidence for Life After Death* (HarperSanFrancisco, a division of HarperCollins

Publishers, New York, 1992). (First published in Great Britain by BBC Books.)

Jackson, Herbert G. Jr., *The Spirit Rappers: The Strange Story of Kate and Maggie Fox, Founders of the American Spiritualist Movement* (Garden City, New York, Doubleday & Company, 1972)

Johnson, Raynor C., *The Imprisoned Splendour: An Approach to Reality, Based upon the Significance of Data Drawn from the Fields of Natural Science, Psychical Research and Mystical Experience* (New York, Harper & Brothers, 1953)

Jordan, Ralph D., *Psychic Counselor's Handbook: Ethics, Tools, and Techniques* (Kailua-Kona, Hawaii, Inner Perceptions, Inc., 1999)

Jung, C. G., *Memories, Dreams, Reflections* (New York, Pantheon Books, 1961). Recorded and edited by Aneila Jaffe. Translated from the German by Richard and Clara Winston.

Kaku, Michio, *Hyperspace* (Oxford Paperbacks, Reissue October, 1995)

Karagulla, Shafica, *Breakthrough to Creativity: Your Higher Sense Perception* (Santa Monica, California, DeVorss & Co., 1967)

Kardec, Allan, *The Book on Mediums: Guide for Mediums and Invocators* (York Beach, Maine, Samuel Weiser, Inc., 1970). First published in 1874. *The Spirits' Book*, Albuquerque (New Mexico, Brotherhood of Life, Inc., 1989). Revised edition first published in 1857.

Keene, M Lamar, as told to Allen Spraggett, *The Psychic Mafia* (New York, Prometheus Books, 1997). Originally published (New York, St. Martin's Press, 1976)

Kerr, Howard, *Mediums and Spirit-Rappers and Roaring Radicals: Spiritualism in American Literature 1850–1900* (Chicago, University of Illinois Press, 1972)

Kilner, Walter J., *The Human Aura* (Secaucus, New York, Citadel Press, 1965)

Kitzman, Elizabeth, *A Chosen Vessel* (DeVorss)

Klimo, Jon, *Channeling: Investigations on Receiving Information from Paranormal Sources* (Berkeley, California, North Atlantic Books, 1998)

Krippner, Stanley, Editor, *Advances in Parapsychological Research 5* (Jefferson, N.C., McFarland & Co., 1987)

Krippner, Stanley. Editor. *Advances in Parapsychological Research 4* (Jefferson, N.C., McFarland & Co., 1984)

Krippner, Stanley. Editor. *Advances in Parapsychological Research 3* (New York, Plenum Press, 1982)

Krippner, Stanley. Editor. *Advances in Parapsychological Research 2: Extrasensory Perception* (New York, Plenum Press, 1978)

Krippner, Stanley. Editor. *Advances in Parapsychological Research 1: Psychokinesis* (New York, Plenum Press, 1977)

Kubler-Ross, Elizabeth, *On Death and Dying*

Kubler-Ross, Elizabeth, *Questions and Answers on Death and Dying*

Kubler-Ross, Elizabeth, *Living with Death and Dying* (Souvenir Press, London 1998) LaGrand, Louis E., *After Death Communication Final Farewells: Extraordinary Experiences of Those Mourning the Death of Loved Ones* (St. Paul, Minnesota, Llewellyn, 1997)

Lang, J Stephen, *1,001 Things You Always Wanted To Know about Angels, Demons and the Afterlife, But Never Thought To Ask* (Thomas Nelson Publishers, October 2000)

Langley, Noel, *Edgar Cayce on Reincarnation* (New York, Warner Books, 1967)

Leek, Sybil, *Telepathy: The 'Respectable' Phenomenon* (New York, The Macmillan Company, 1971)

Leshan, Lawrence, *The Medium, the Mystic, and the Physicist* (New York, Viking Press, 1966)

Lundegaard, Karen A., *A Hare Krishna Community: Personality and Life-Style Differences Between the Male and Female Members* (Ann Arbor, Michigan: University Microfilms, 1986)

MacGregor, Geddes, *Angels: Ministers of Grace* (New York, Paragon, 1988)

MacDonald, William L., *Idionecrophanies: The Social Construction of Perceived Contact with the Dead, Journal for the Scientific Study of Religion* (31(2): 215–223) 1992.

Manford, Mark, Andermann F., *Complex Visual Hallucinations. Clinical and Neurobiological Insights* [Review] in Brain 121 pt.10, October 1998)

Marcotte, Armand, and Ann Druffel. *Past Lives, Future Growth* (Norfolk, Virginia, Hampton Roads, 1984, 1993)

Marris, P., *Widows and their Families* (London, RKP, 1958)

Martin, Joel, and Patricia Romanowski *Our Children Forever: George Anderson's Messages from Children on the Other Side* (New York, Berkley, 1994)

Martin, Joel, and Patricia Romanowski *Love Beyond Life: The Healing Power of After-Death Communications*

Martin-Kuri, K.A, *Message for the Millennium* (New York, Ballantine Books, 1996) *We Are Not Forgotten: George Anderson's Messages of Hope from the Other Side* (New York, Putnam, 1991; Berkley, 1992) *We Don't Die: George Anderson's Conversations with the Other Side* (New York, Putnam, 1988; Berkley, 1989)

Maynard, Nettie Colburn, *Was Abraham Lincoln a Spiritualist? Or, Curious Revelations from the Life of a Trance Medium* (Chicago, The Progressive Thinker Publishing House, 1917). (First edition was published in 1891.)

McClain, Florence Wagner, *A Practical Guide to Past Life Regression* (St. Paul, Minnesota, Llewellyn Publications, 1988)

Meek, George W., *After We Die, What Then? Evidence You Will Live Forever!* (Atlanta, Georgia, Ariel Press, 1987)

Meek, George W. *Enjoy Your Own Funeral and Live a Happy Forever* (Lakeville, Minnesota, Galde Press, 1999)

Metzner, Ralph, *Maps of Consciousness* (New York, Collier Books, 1971)

Moody, Raymond. *Reunions: Visionary Encounters with Departed Loved Ones* (New York, Random House, 1993)

Moody, Raymond, *Life After Life* (New York, Mockingbird Books, 1975)

Moody, Raymond with Paul Perry, *Reunions: Visionary Encounters with Departed Loved Ones* (Warner Books, London, 1995)

Moore, W. Usborne, *Glimpses of the Next State: The Education of an Agnostic* (London, Watts & Co., 1911)

Morse, Melvin, with Paul Perry, *Closer to the Light: Learning from the Near-Death Experiences of Children* (New York, Ballantine Books, 1990)

Morse, Melvin, *Parting Visions*

Murphy, Gardner, and Robert O. Ballou, compilers and editors. *William James on Psychical Research* (New York, Viking Press, 1960)

Murphy, Michael, *The Future of the Body: Explorations Into the Further Evolution of Human Nature*, (New York, Jeremy P. Tarcher/Putnam, 1992)

Myer-Czetli, Nancy, and Steve N. Czetli, *Silent Witness: The Story of a Psychic Detective* (New York, Birch Lane/Carol Publishing Group, 1993)

Myers, F. W. H., *Human Personality and Its Survival of Bodily Death*. Vols. 1 & 2. (Longmans, Green, 1903, 1954)

Nash, Carroll B., *Science of PSI ESP and PK* (Springfield, Illinois, Charles C. Thomas Publisher, 1978)

Newton, Michael, *Destiny of Souls: New Cases of Life Between Lives* (St. Paul, Minnesota, Llewellyn Publications, 2000)

Nichols, Beverley, *Powers That Be* (London, Jonathan Cape, 1966)

Northrop, Suzane, with Kate McLoughlin, *Séance: A Guide for the Living* (New York, Alliance Publishing, 1994)

Ostrander, Sheila, and Lynn Schroeder, *Handbook of PSI Discoveries* (New York, Berkley Publishing Corporation, 1974)

Pagels, Elaine, *The Origin of Satan* (New York, Random House, 1995) *Psychic Discoveries Behind the Iron Curtain* (Englewood Cliffs, New Jersey, Prentice-Hall, 1970)

Parkes, C.M., *Bereavement and Mental Illness* (British Journal of Medical Psychology, 38, 1) (1965).

Parkes, C.M., and R.S. Weiss, *Recovery from Bereavement* (Basic Books, New York, 1983)

Perez, Maya, with Terry Latterman, *Born with a Veil: The Life of a Spiritual Mystic* (Norfolk, Virginia, Hampton Roads Publishing Company, 1991)

Phillips, C. Doreen, *The Autobiography of a Fortune Teller* (New York, Vantage Press, 1958)

Pike, James A., with Diane Kennedy, *The Other Side: An Account of My Experiences with Psychic Phenomena* (Garden City, New York, Doubleday & Company, 1968)

Podmore, Frank, *Mediums of the 19th Century.* Vol. 1 (New Hyde Park, New York, University Books, 1963). First published in 1902.

Pollack, Jack Harrison, *Croiset the Clairvoyant* (New York, Doubleday & Company, 1964)

Pond, Mariam Buckner, *The Unwilling Martyrs: The Story of the Fox Family* (London, Spiritualist Press, 1947)

Prince, Walter Franklin, *The Case of Patience Worth* (New Hyde Park, New York, University Books, 1964)

Psychics: In-depth Interviews. Edited by the editors of Psychic Magazine (New York, Harper & Row, 1972)

Radin, Dean, *The Conscious Universe: The Scientific Truth of Psychic Phenomena* (San Francisco, HarperEdge, 1997)

Raudive, Konstantin, *Breakthrough: An Amazing Experiment in Electronic Communication with the Dead*. Translated by Nadia Fowler (Gerrards Cross, Buckinghamshire, Colin Smythe Limited, 1971)

Ritzer, George, *The McDonaldization of Society* (Pine Forge Press, 1996)

Robb, Stewart, ed. *True Spirit Stories* (New York, Pyramid Books, 1969)

Roberts, Estelle, *Fifty Years a Medium* (London, Corgi Books, 1969)

Ronan, Margaret, *Strange, Unsolved Mysteries* (Scholastic Book Service, 1974)

St. Clair, David, *The Psychic World of California* (New York, Doubleday & Company, 1972)

Schultz, G., Needham, W., Taylor, R., Shindell, S., Melzack, R., *Properties of Complex Hallucinations Associated with Deficits in Vision in Perception* 25(6), 1996.

Schwartz, Gary E. R., and Linda G. S. Russek. *The Living Energy Universe: A Fundamental Discovery that Transforms Science & Medicine* (Charlottesville, Virginia, Hampton Roads, 1999).

Shelton, Harriet M., *Abraham Lincoln Returns* (New York, The Evans Publishing Company, 1957)

Sherman, Harold M., *The Dead Are Alive: They Can and Do Communicate with You* (New York, Ballantine, 1981); *You Live After Death* (New York, Creative Age Press, 1950)

Shroder, Tom, *Old Souls: The Scientific Evidence for Past Lives* (New York, Simon & Schuster, 1999)

Smith, A. Robert (Compiler/Editor), *The Lost Memoirs of Edgar Cayce: Life as a Seer* (Virginia Beach, VA, A.R.E. Press, 1997)

Smith, Eleanor Touhey, *Psychic People* (New York, William Morrow, 1968)

Smith, Penelope, *Animal Talk: Interspecies Telepathic Communication* (Point Reyes Station, California, Pegasus Publications, 1989). First published as *Animal Talk – A Guide to Communicating With and Understanding Animals*, 1982.

Smith, Susy, *The Afterlife Codes: Searching for Evidence of the Survival of the Soul* (Charlottesville, Virginia, Hampton Roads, 2000)

Smith, Susy, *Life Is Forever: Evidence for Survival After Death* (New York, G. P. Putnam's Sons, 1974) *The Mediumship of Mrs. Leonard* (New Hyde Park, New York, University Books, 1964)

Soloman, G., and J., *The Schole Experiment: Scientific Evidence for Life after Death* (Piatkus, London, 1999)

Spraggett, Allen, with William V. Rauscher. *Arthur Ford: The Man Who Talked with the Dead* (New York, New American Library, 1973)

Stearn, Jess, *A Matter of Immortality: Dramatic Evidence of Survival* (New York, Atheneum, 1976); *Edgar Cayce: The Sleeping Prophet The Miracle Workers: America's Psychic Consultants* (Garden City, New York, Doubleday & Company, 1972)

Stemman, Roy, *The Supernatural: Spirits and Spirit Worlds* (London, Aldus Books, 1975)

Stevenson, Ian, *Children Who Remember Previous Lives: A Question of Reincarnation*. Revised Edition, (McFarland & Company, 2000)

Stevenson, Ian, *Where Reincarnation and Biology Intersect* (Westport, Connecticut, Praeger Publishers, 1997)

Stevenson, Ian, *Twenty Cases Suggestive of Reincarnation* (New York, American Society for Psychical Research, 1966)

Sugrue, Thomas, *There Is a River: The Story of Edgar Cayce* (New York, Holt, Rinehart and Winston, 1942)
Swedenborg, Emmanuel.
Tabori, Paul, *Crime and the Occult: How ESP and Parapsychology Help Detection* (New York, Taplinger Publishing Co., 1974)

Taylor, R.E., Mancil, G.L., Kramer, S.H., *Visual Hallucinations: Meaning and Management in Journal of the American Optomeric Association* 57(12) December 1986, pp. 889–92.

Tietze, Thomas R., *Margery* (New York, Harper & Row, 1973)
Time-Life Books, Editors, *Mysteries of the Unknown* (Alexandria, Virginia, TIME-LIFE BOOKS, 1992). This series examines the history and nature of seemingly paranormal phenomena. The books in the series include: *Alien Encounters; Ancient Wisdom and Secret Sects; Cosmic Connections; Cosmic Duality; Dreams and Dreaming; Earth Energies; Eastern Mysteries; Hauntings; Magical Arts; Master Index and Illustrated Symbols; The Mind and Beyond; Mind over Matter; Mysterious Creatures; Mysterious Lands and Peoples; The Mysterious World; Mystic Places; Mystic Quests; The Mystical Year; Phantom Encounters; Powers of Healing; Psychic Powers; Psychic Voyages; Search for Immortality; Search for the Soul; Secrets of the Alchemists; Spirit Summonings; Time and Space; Transformations; The UFO Phenomenon; Utopian Visions; Visions and Prophecies; Witches and Witchcraft.*

Tompkins, Peter, and Christopher Bird. *The Secret Life of Plants* (New York, Harper & Row, 1973)

Twigg, Ena, with Ruth Hagy Brod. *Ena Twigg: Medium* (New York, Hawthorn Books, 1972)

Van Praagh, James, *Healing Grief: Reclaiming Life After Any Loss* (New York, Dutton, 2000) *Reaching to Heaven: A Spiritual Journey Through Life and Death* (New York, Dutton, 1999) *Talking to Heaven: A Medium's Message of Life After Death* (New York, Dutton, 1997)

Vasiliev, Leonid L., *Mysterious Phenomena of the Human Psyche*. Translated by Sonia Volochova (New Hyde Park, New York, University Books, 1965)

Virtue, Doreen, *Divine Guidance: How to Have Conversations with God and Your Guardian*

Vishita, Bhakta. *Genuine Mediumship: The Invisible Powers* (Desplaines, Illinois, Yoga Publication Society, 1919)

Vlasek, Mary C., *Handbook of the Phenomena and Philosophy of Mediumship*.

Wallis, E. W. and M. H. Wallis, *A Guide to Mediumship and Psychical Unfoldment* (Mokelumne Hill, California, Health Research, 1968). Reprint. Original publication date unknown.

Warrick, F. W., *Experiments in Psychics: Practical Studies in Direct Writing, Supernormal Photography, and Other Phenomena Mainly with Mrs. Ada Emma Deane* (New York, E. P. Dutton & Co., 1939)

Weiss, Brian L., *Many Lives, Many Masters* (New York, A Fireside Book, Simon & Schuster, 1988)

Wheeler, David R., *Journey to the Other Side* (New York, Ace Books/Grosset & Dunlop Company, 1976)

White, Stewart Edward, *The Betty Book: Excursions into the World of Other-Consciousness Made by Betty between 1919 and 1936* (New York, E. P. Dutton & Company, 1937)

Wilkins,_, and Harold Sherman, *Thoughts Through Space*.

Wolman, Benjamin B., Editor, *Handbook of Parapsychology* (New York, Van Nostrand Reinhold Company, 1977)

Woods, Walter, with Marin Gazzaniga, *Powers That Be* (Hugh Lauter Levin Associates, 2000)

Worrall, Ambrose A., with Olga N. Worrall, *The Gift of Healing: A Personal Story of Spiritual Therapy* (New York, Harper & Row, 1965)

Zolar. *Zolar's Book of the Spirits* (New York, Prentice Hall Press, 1987)

'*WHAT MOST PEOPLE BELIEVE TO BE THE OTHER SIDE
I CONSIDER HOME ... WE ARE ALL JUST WORKING OUR WAY BACK*'

SAM DI PAOLA

BIOGRAPHY

EMMA HEATHCOTE-JAMES WAS born in Harborne, Birmingham in 1977. Whilst still at school, she became interested in the phenomenon of religion which led to a degree in Theology at the University of Birmingham with research findings from her undergraduate studies in religious experience extended to a Masters degree and then the PhD from which a BBC *Everyman* documentary and her first bestselling book *Seeing Angels* arose. From this stemmed *After Death Communication* and her third book *They Walk Among Us*.

Over the past few years Emma has been a guest on Radio 4's *Women's Hour*, TalkSPORT, BBC World and Radio 2's *Johnnie Walker* show on several occasions, has presented papers at various conferences, seminars and journals as well as having contributed to numerous international and national TV programmes (*BBC Heaven and Earth*, *Horizon*, *Britain's Most Haunted Live*, *This Morning*, *Open House* etc) on the subject of religion and paranormal phenomena. Emma's main interests lie in the field of anthropology of religion and the psychology behind why people believe in the things they do. She is intrigued by visions and experiences and has a vast and unparalled database of firsthand contemporary testimonies. She has researched numerous experiences including stigmata, alien encounters, simulacrums, visions of angels, Jesus, the BVM and other alleged miracles across the world.

Emma moved into the area of religious broadcasting straight after her degree, then moved into more primetime television slots, with recent credits including *ITV's Star Lives*, *Soap Star Lives*, Channel 4's *Perfect Match* and two commissioned short films for Carlton Television. She now spends more time writing and working in PR and lives in a cottage in the North Cotswolds.

OTHER BOOKS BY THE AUTHOR

SEEING ANGELS
Blake Publishing Ltd; ISBN: 1904034152
For three years, Emma researched a phenomenon that had not, as yet, been studied seriously. Hundreds of British people have claimed to have experienced visions of angels. These people are not crazy new-age loonies, but ordinary people from all walks of life, from professionals to prisoners to children. Emma is a theology graduate whose PhD research into contemporary experiences of angels is re-written here into layman's terms. Her findings are groundbreaking and unique, and include more than 350 fascinating accounts which she has analysed in depth.

THEY WALK AMONG US
Metro Publishing Ltd; ISBN: 1843580977
This book contains the best scientific evidence yet collected for the reality of life after death. It challenges the accepted ideas of exactly what we are and what we become after death. Written for the enquirer, layman and accustomed reader alike, it looks in-

depth at the one, little-known phenomena – physical or materialisation mediumship – which can seemingly prove there is an afterlife after all. It describes how experiments can induce 'spirits' of deceased relatives to manifest in solid forms within a séance setting and walk about the room. For the first time Ronald Pearson's suppressed physics and mathematical formulae is published which backs it all up, showing such a phenomenon to be a natural law rather than something improbable or in the realms of parapsychology.

The extensive research collects interviews and reports collated by Heathcote-James, the first journalist in over 20 years, outside of spiritualism, to analyse and detail the astonishing and so rare phenomena of materialisation and describes how objects are being passed from the spirit world. She has also been allowed to witness these animated images from other realms on sealed video, hear voices caught on audio cassettes and see them captured on photographic material. Written with an open and enquiring mind, this radical thesis is for people who are willing to cast aside traditional, religious and orthodox notions of the afterlife and spirit world. This book may alter your views, explaining a theory that perhaps an afterlife could logically exist after all. Seemingly everything can now be rationally explained in physics, facilitating astounding new and as some claim, conclusive evidence of survival after death. The findings within these pages can only bring comfort and lessen fear of the next world and is a staple read for anyone looking to explore more deeply their inner self and move forward in their quest to finding the truth.